The Ninth of November

The Ninth of November

Hannele Zürndorfer

Quartet Books
London Melbourne New York

First Published by Quartet Books Limited 1983
A member of the Namara Group
27/29 Goodge Street, London W1P 1FD

British Library Cataloguing in Publication Data

Zürndorfer, Hannele
  The ninth of November.
  1. Zürndorfer, Hannele   2. Jews—Germany—
  Biography
  I. Title
  943'.004924   DS135.E33

  ISBN 0-7043-2376-1

Typeset by MC Typeset, Rochester, Kent
Printed in Great Britain by Nene Litho
and bound by Woolnough Bookbinding, both of Wellingborough, Northants

This book is dedicated to the memory of my parents, but I hope that it may also serve as an acknowledgement of the steadfastness of those people in Germany who never succumbed to the poison of National Socialism, and of the generosity of the people of Britain, my second country and now my first.

Contents

Illustrations

Preface

What follows is an account of my early life in Germany in the 1930s and in wartime Britain.

I have described my experiences as I remember them, and since the politics of the period affected me – like so many others – profoundly, the book is incidentally an account of great events impinging on ordinary people, and seen through the eyes of a child.

It will appear that I was an indulged child who idolized her father. I was, and I did. I will only add that the father I have described is the father I remember – and I have been impressed by the extent to which others who knew him have subsequently confirmed my impression of an extraordinary man.

Fife, 1982

1 Beginnings

I was born on St Nicholas Day 1925, which, my father said, was a good day to be born, because it was the hundredth anniversary of Marlitt's birth. I never found out much about Marlitt, except that he was a writer. I arrived quite early in my parents' marriage, probably because my father, who was fifty when I was born, felt under some pressure of time. My mother was twenty-five and his niece.

The oddity of this relationship, which involved two generations, delighted my father, who enjoyed disconcerting people with it and puzzling me and my sister by assuring us that we were our own cousins. It arose because my father had been married before to a girl called Klara Weinheim, and my mother was the daughter of Klara's half-sister.

People who knew her described Klara as beautiful and cultured and very much in love with my father. That she was in fact beautiful I know from her portrait and photographs, and that my father adored her, his poems, letters and diary extracts bear out. After barely a year of marriage Klara contracted tuberculosis and remained an invalid for the rest of her life, looked after with devotion by my father, but unable to have children. My mother, Else, helped to nurse her in the last stages of her illness. Klara died after twenty years of marriage when my father was forty-eight.

'If you marry again, marry Else,' was her dying advice to my father. And he took it. It may have been in Klara's mind that my mother's open, generous nature and her youth would give my father something he had lacked and the children he so much wanted. He always explained to us that after twenty years of marriage he suddenly found himself *ein Mann ohne Sorgen* (a man without cares), which was uninteresting and so he married my mother, had children and cares, and was happy again.

My mother admired my father enormously. During her adolescence she seems to have found the infrequent visits of Adolf and Klara to her home in Alsace very exciting; she clearly found her uncle-by-marriage more understanding than her rather unimaginative parents, and when, a year after Klara's death, my father actually asked her to marry him, she was overwhelmed. Her parents were keen to encourage this advantageous match, but my father said that it was not really fair to hurry an inexperienced girl, half his age, into binding herself to him. He insisted that for one year they did not see each other, while my mother made up her mind about so serious a step.

In the meantime, another of Klara's half-sisters, maiden aunt Minna, let it be known that she felt better suited to 'take care of dear Adolf' and cruised from branch to branch of the family demonstrating her claim, but at the end of the year my mother decided to take up her option, so that was that. In October 1924 Adolf Zürndorfer and Elisabeth Dorothea Rheinheimer married and spent a carefree honeymoon in the mountains of Switzerland.

With her provincial background and her untutored mind, my mother must have found the life to which my father introduced her in Düsseldorf glamorous and exciting, but a little daunting. He was at that time managing director of a publishing firm, Ed. Lintz, as well as the drama critic on the *Frankfurter Zeitung* for the Düsseldorfer Stadttheater, covering also many of the exciting premieres for the *Theaterwelt*.

My mother was suddenly whirled on visits to theatres, operas, concerts and thrust into the company of writers, actors, artists and musicians – Kurt Heynicke, Herbert Eulenberg, Karl Röttger, Louise Dumont, Walter Opey are names I was always hearing as a child, and my mother must have wondered how she could ever measure up to their demands. When we used to ask my father, as children often do, 'What made you marry Mummy?' he would look at her gently and smile and say,

'Because she is such a good listener.' I think I have remembered this because it seemed to me then such an odd answer, not wholly satisfying, but intriguing.

In our sitting-room there hung a large oil painting of Klara in a white dress. I didn't know then that my father had been married before, but I wondered why flowers were placed beside the portrait on a certain day each year. Who was this Klara and why was she so important that her birthday should be honoured with floral tributes? Perhaps it was because of the evasive answers to my insistent questions that I slightly resented these flowers, although my mother did not seem to mind. But later, when I saw Klara's portrait slashed to pieces, my horror and shock were vaguely mingled with a certain guilty satisfaction. But by then I was twelve, and it may have had more to do with my growing up than with my parents' relationship. Certainly when I was five or six there was no flaw in their fondness for each other. My father used to come home for the midday meal – the big meal of the day – and after it, he and Mummy would lie down side by side on the rather narrow chaise-longue in the sitting-room with a brown travelling rug over them for a little siesta. My sister and I used to be sent into our room to play, but in some indefinable way I remember feeling pleased and reassured to see them lying so closely curled up under the brown rug. After the siesta and a cup of strong black coffee my father returned to the office to work, often till quite late in the evening. Or he might stay in town and go on to the theatre after work without coming home in between. I don't remember exactly when these tender siestas stopped, but I do remember thinking one day that they had stopped. I always loved that brown rug.

Until I was five we lived in the Hermannstrasse, a quiet, residential street, twenty minutes by tram from the centre of Düsseldorf. Our flat was on the first floor. It was quite big, but had no garden to speak of – just a front patch with sky-blue hydrangeas. I think it was in those days that my father joined the *Schrebergartenverein* – a garden club, but it was not like an English allotment. It meant that we rented a large garden on the outskirts of the town and paid a gardener to grow vegetables and soft fruit and to keep the lawn and flowerbeds in order. I don't think we went there nearly often enough – it was quite an excursion by tram, laden with picnic-baskets and other paraphernalia. I recall several happy occasions when either my mother, Änne, the maid, and I, or the whole family clan – *die ganze Mischpoche*! as my father would ruefully remark – went to picnic and gather in the harvest. There was a blue and red summer-house with a large round table and deckchairs; there was even a swing and a sandpit. My father, in relaxed mood, for once without his stiff Victorian collar, went around proudly as though he himself had been responsible for all this fruitfulness. I remember Daddy laughing happily as we squealed over the delights of picking strawberries, or cherries or redcurrants. He used to disappear among the blackcurrant bushes whose harsh flavour he preferred to all others. Even today the astringent smell of marigolds, the amber velvet of wallflowers or the peacock splendour of sweet william awaken memories of that garden; delectable lunches coming out of mysteriously wrapped boxes and jars; potato salad, tomatoes and cold meats and heavenly raspberry juice; everybody happy and chatting round the big table. And so the afternoon passed, golden and green. Then coffee out of thermos flasks, and there was cake, and towards sunset in summer when the midges started dancing, we would return laden with beans and peas, cherries and strawberries and flowers.

Of the Hermannstrasse flat I have only the dimmest recollections. I do clearly recall being encouraged to put lumps of sugar outside on the windowsill, so that the stork could take them away and bring me a little sister. I have a vague picture of Änne, my father and me placing the sugar-lumps one morning after break-fast and of the general astonishment, when next morning they had gone. I was amazed, but at the same time a little dissatisfied; I don't know whether it was because I didn't actually see the stork take the sugar, or because I doubted the explanation. In any case, the interval between sugar and sister was far too long.

Next I remember visiting Mummy in the nursing home. I was also allowed to view my little sister, but remember nothing of her at that stage. I was more interested in Mummy's lunch. I couldn't really fathom what Mummy was doing there in that strange bed. I supposed it had something to do with my little sister and I resented her being there, instead of being at home with me and I have a picture of her trying to meet my fierce resentment gently, with her black hair sprawling all over the place.

I had been told that the sister would be for me, but very soon I learnt differently. She was actually treated as a person in her own right! I wasn't even allowed to dress and undress her, as I did my

4

dolls. I felt very let down. I am told I was fiercely jealous and on one occasion was only just stopped in time from pouring scalding milk over her. Apparently I became very contrary and disobedient. Once, when I was being a nuisance in the kitchen and persisting in playing with the eggs, my Uncle Ala, who was visiting us and who prided himself on his whimsical sense of humour, suggested I should throw them on the floor – confident, no doubt, that I would perversely do no such thing – but on that occasion I was obedient, which got Ala into trouble.

Around 1930, when I was four, we moved to Gerresheim on the outskirts of Düsseldorf. It was about three-quarters of an hour by tram from the centre of town, and what appealed to my father was the countrified atmosphere of the place and the wooded hills that he always referred to as the *Gerresheimer Schweiz*. He often walked there by himself, and on Sunday mornings he took us there while Mummy cooked the dinner.

Ours was a large corner house with the special attraction of a romantic turret, overgrown with a wild vine that turned a heady burgundy in autumn. The house was divided, as is common in Germany, and formed two large flats and a smaller attic one. We took the ground floor and let the other two. There wasn't much of a garden, only a front garden with lovely deep blue hydrangeas (as in the Hermannstrasse) and a rather shady back garden with much flagging and stonework, as I remember it, and not much grass. There was, however, a sandpit, a large ornamental pond and fountain without water. As the house was on a corner, its share of garden got squeezed away, and on the south side it dwindled to a mere path between narrow flowerbeds, ending in a small shrubbery. This was my father's favourite spot for taking photographs, for if we were placed judiciously in front of the shrubbery, it gave an impression of leafy parklands stretching away into the distance.

During the move to Gerresheim I was sent to stay with my Aunt Rosa in Ohligs, about two hours by train. Her husband, a cousin of my father's, had been killed in the First World War, and she managed the large drapery store alone, with regular advice from my father. I remember my visit well. For one thing it was my first independent railway journey (I have the ticket still, dated 18 March 1930) and I felt very proud. Daddy put me on the train at Düsseldorf and asked a kindly lady to keep an eye on me. I had no misgivings, but felt excited and adventurous. At the other end I was met by my aunt and my twenty-year-old cousin, Margot.

I enjoyed my stay enormously, particularly because I was sometimes allowed to help in the shop. I remember so well coming down from breakfast in the large first-floor flat, into the bright shop and being assailed by the exciting smell of new fabric. The five or six assistants would be busy stacking and sorting, arranging and checking, before the shop opened and I would be able to wander behind the glass-topped counters that ran the length of the shop on either side, looking through the glass at the elaborate display of artificial flowers (fashionable in those days for embellishing evening dresses, suits and hats); there were pale green silk roses, pink camelias, black-petalled peonies. I gazed at the shiny satin lingerie, the lace-trimmed petticoats and nighties, at white, gauzy gloves, tucked collars and cuffs.

Along the wall ran rows of drawers and shelves stacked with heavy rolls of materials. I loved the brisk efficiency with which the assistants handled them, suddenly flooding the counter with a river of blue, or a shimmering green meadow and then that marvellous ripping sound as the sharp scissors sliced swiftly and cleanly through the fabric.

Stacked along one section from floor to ceiling were shiny white cardboard boxes containing an endless variety of buttons, each box with one sample-button sewn on the front. There were cards of silky fringes for curtains and lampshades, bindings and trimmings, cotton reels of every hue, drawers full of ribbons – velvet, satin or ribbed grosgrain – in every shade imaginable. My chief delight, however, was to watch the senior assistant making cloth-covered buttons to order on the manual button machine. She used to give me all sorts of bright bits and pieces and my precious hoard of colourful oddments grew day by day. The acme of my stay was when I was actually allowed to serve a customer – obviously a friend of my aunt's.

'Can I help you, Madam?' I asked, just as I had heard the assistants do.

'Yes please, could you show me some white summer gloves,' she replied, quite seriously as though I were a new assistant, even though I topped the counter by only a few inches. My joy was complete when she actually bought a pair.

There was no garden at Ohligs, but for my benefit a swing had been hung in the spacious passage of the flat. My room had been brightened and made interesting with old toys and books of Margot's; there was one of those prim-looking, jointed china dolls, rather fragile and ailing and I could not imagine how Margot had ever found her companionable. But Margot herself was a lovely person, soft and gentle with full lips and dimpled cheeks. She read to me and played with me and took me for walks and visits to friends. I recall falling asleep at night in a room all to myself (at home I had to share with my sister) and hearing on the edge of night, as it seemed, the rhythmical chuffing of a train, drawing further and further away, and I used to try and catch the last wisp of sound and then a sort of contented mysterious sigh came from the night outside, just as I fell asleep.

Then one day Daddy walked into the shop to take me home. Though I was sorry my visit was at an end, I was to go home to our new house – that too was a delightful prospect. In my memory of the Sonnbornstrasse (which means street of the sun's source) our rooms were always sunny and light and the street was lined with plane trees with jigsaw puzzle trunks, which we peeled until they looked quite naked. There began for us children a time that I remember as utterly happy and carefree.

My father was usually gay and happy in those days, and so was I. I think I must always have been greatly influenced by what he felt and I seemed to sense his mood, however much he tried to hide his worries from us in the days to come. Sometimes in later years I would sense an almost tangible blackness in him, which, in turn, filled me with a bleak feeling, almost of choking. There is a strange image in my mind of the dinner-table with a brilliantly white cloth on it and my father standing at the head of it (my mother and sister are there, but only as shadows) and I am standing beside him, unable to speak or cry, but fit to burst with an uncomprehended misery. But all that was in the future. At this time my father used to sing and laugh, and roam through the woods with us and run down the hills, with us squealing on either side.

We children had a large room with a raised bay, reached by a step up, making it like a stage, which was useful for our play-acting games. We looked out on to the Lacronstrasse and more plane trees. We had many toys and books, a rocking-horse and a beautifully carved doll's house, made by a cousin of my father's in true Bavarian style: the furniture painted bright blue with white and red flowers on the chair-backs, bedheads, chests and cupboards and little hearts cut out of the wood. One birthday I was given a desk with an ink-well and a stool to match; that became a cherished possession and no one was allowed to open the lid after I had lost the key. A doll called Ruth I remember with great affection, rosy-cheeked with dark plaits, long eyelashes and blue eyes that opened and shut, then still a novelty.

Of the many books there were some favourites: one I was particularly fond of when I was small, because it had beautiful illustrations of anthropormorphic flowers and toadstools. Several (inevitably, in Germany) concerned gnomes and elves who lived in dark pinewoods, also inhabited by gruesome witches. There were the deliciously frightening stories of the Brothers Grimm, Hauff and Brentano. One picture, illustrating Goethe's children's story called 'The Golden Pot', showed a terrified man under a large oak from which hundreds of green snakes were squirming and reaching out at him, and the sky was a dark green. There was 'Sternenfritzchen', about little Fritz who had been dropped from a star and had many odd adventures on earth before he was able to return. A little later I was an inveterate consumer of the 'Nesthäckchen' books, a series of twelve volumes, which followed the career of a little girl called Annemie Braun, the youngest of three in a doctor's family in Berlin, from her nursery-school days in 1900 right through to university in Tübingen and marriage. Because these books were so popular, Else Ury, the author, wrote another two volumes about Nesthäckchen as mother and grandmother. I suppose the 'Katy' books are our nearest equivalent.

But gradually emerging, better than all the books and toys, was my sister Lotte. Though she was three and a half years younger, I drilled her until she was adept at all kinds of pretence games, some with very complicated rules. Of course, like most little girls we loved playing *Schicke Damen* (posh ladies), dressing up in Mummy's high-heeled shoes, hats, carrying old leather handbags with mirrors, powder-compacts and combs. We would act out our meetings at cafés and *Konditoreien* on our 'stage', sipping water from the dolls' tea-set, opening and shutting our handbags endlessly and conducting the sort of inane conversations we imagined posh ladies to indulge in.

We had one special 'talking' game at night, when we were supposed to be going to sleep. Many a time Mummy would have to come in. 'What, are you still talking? Not another word now!'

Then, after a little silence we would start up again, at first in whispers, then getting more and more animated, until the next visitation.

Until I went to school I don't recall any special friends of my own. Lotte and I did everything together. She was a dainty person with enormous brown eyes and dark curls. There was an appealing quality about her, which I sometimes resented when it helped to get her out of trouble. I was able to dominate her up to a point in those days, but already she had a strong will of her own and any frustrations caused a sudden outburst of temper. In the last resort she would complain of my wickednesses to Mummy, and I, as the elder, was often blamed for what *I* considered to be the fault of both of us.

As the dethroned child, I was far more anxious for affection and reassurance than she was. In fact, at one stage I was constantly asking Mummy and Daddy, 'Do you love me? Do you love me more than Lotte?' or 'Do you love me forever and ever, whatever I do?' This would go on until even their patience was exhausted and they would say, 'If you go on like this, people will get fed up with you.' 'But you're not fed up yet, are you? You still love me as much as you did before I started asking?'

I needed hugging and kissing and constant reassurance. Perhaps, besides natural childish reactions, I had sensed the insecurity that was already seeping through Germany like marsh vapour.

But though I was often deeply jealous of any attention and affection directed at Lotte, and though we often squabbled noisily, we were, in fact, very fond of each other. I have always felt very protective towards her: ready to bully and attack her myself, but fierce in her defence against outsiders. This was well, for in later days we needed each other.

2 Origins

As young children we loved nothing better than to hear my father
tell stories of his own childhood and he never had to be asked
twice. He was born in the village of Jebenhausen in Swabia in
1874, the second in a family of four surviving children. There had
been seven: two had died in infancy and Klärle died at the age of
six – 'a great sorrow to us all' – but she had been 'too good to live'.

Max was the eldest, then came my father, Adolf, then Hugo
and lastly Rosel, who was eight years younger than my father.
Always a family-conscious man, my father had drawn up a family
tree going back to the seventeenth century. I can't remember any
details, but he often showed it to us proudly, telling us stories
about the separate branches. Apparently our ancestors fled from
Spain during the Inquisition and in the thirteenth century settled
in a village in the south of Germany which is still called Zürndorf
and where there are (or were until the last war) many family
graves. Sometimes my father would make a pilgrimage to the
village and visit the graves, trying to decipher the faded Hebrew
inscriptions. The old family house where his great-grandmother
had been born was still standing somewhere near Zürndorf in
1938, when he went there for the last time.

Somewhere, not too far back on my grandmother's side, there
had been the inevitable black sheep: a musician who gave lessons
at the local manor and had an affair with the gentile daughter of
the house. I don't know if they actually eloped, but he married

her. Hence, so my father rather proudly pointed out, the blue-eyed and fair-haired streak in our family. He himself had blue-grey eyes and light brown hair, and so have I.

My grandfather, Eduard, moved with his family to a little Swabian village called Dettensee in 1876. There my father spent his childhood and my grandfather ran the village school with the occasional help of a young apprentice teacher. In addition to being schoolmaster, he combined the duties of local rabbi with playing the organ for the village church. My father said his mother was a wonderful woman and wished we could have known her. She was a trained midwife, and in those days of poor medical provision villagers from all round used to come to her about all sorts of trouble and she was never too busy to help.

I have in my possession a packet of mellowed letters, written on pink and mauve paper in faded ink, in beautiful copperplate, dated 1869. They are the letters Eduard Zürndorfer and Jeanette Teilhaber wrote to each other during courtship; they are full of Victorian courtesy and respectful love.

21 April 1869

My dearly cherished Jeanette,

When the heart is filled with emotions never before experienced, it wants to unburden itself by sharing them with another person, but when the person to whom he wants to unburden his heart is not by his side, he has to resort to the pen.

I too, my dear Jeanette, must resort to the pen today, in order to tell you all those things which I was unable to communicate to you in Aalen, partly through sheer excitement, and partly through lack of time.

It is a strange sensation: free one day, engaged the next – but the feeling that has dominated me ever since I have come to know you, is the certainty that I have at last found that which it is often so hard to find. It is a feeling of joy and content that animates me whenever I think of you, and that happens frequently, you may well believe me.

What happiness if you, my dearest one, could think of me in like fashion! How I look forward with longing to your dear lines, which will confirm that you were motivated not by convenience, but by inclination and conviction, when you accepted my proposal. Can you believe me that I am already

11

counting the days which are keeping me apart from you? What sweet happiness it is to love!

I have never before experienced this emotion and therefore the force of these holy desires appears in me with greater power: joyfully and fervently I make this pledge – to offer you everything in my power to make you happy. Will you, my Jeanette, contribute your share to our happiness?

30 April 1869

My dear, good Eduard,

I have just received your dearly cherished letter and I hasten to return my warmest greetings, that I may thereby speed your longingly awaited reply.

Oh! Eduard, how I count every hour until you are with me and through your presence all that which my pen is unable to express – my true and deep love for you – so that we may speak our hearts to each other in the truest sense of this beautiful expression. [Here some lines are omitted.] You asked me for a photograph – I am sorry that at the present moment I cannot grant your request; however, I shall be able to deal with this in our own way. You ask me how old I am, dear Eduard. I will answer you quite precisely: on the day on which I wrote my first letter to you, I was celebrating my 23rd birthday. Now it is your turn!

The names of my father and mother are David and Lea. My dear parents, my brothers and sisters, all of us, are looking forward to your proposed visit. Fanny will be 18 in June, Klara is 15, Josephine 12, Joseph 21 and my little brother Elias is 9.

Now, dear Eduard, be so kind and in your next letter tell me more about your family. I could tell you a great deal more, but am much occupied this week, as my dear mother is away with relatives in Schweinfurt, where she is to be present at the wedding of my cousin to a girl from Würzburg.

Finding myself so happily placed in the circle of my family – my parents, brothers and sisters – I find it doubly hard to think of you being on your own, and often, when we are most happy together, I withdraw quietly so that I may be with you in thought, alone and undisturbed.

Soon you will no longer be alone. I am doing everything I can to hasten that moment.

It was an extremely happy marriage, except that Jeanette died at the age of fifty-five leaving Eduard to continue without her for another twenty years.

Our favourites among my father's stories were those about his schooldays, particularly the pranks of Uncle Hugo. It seems that grandfather Eduard was particularly strict with his own children at school to counter any question of favouritism. Hugo, always in trouble and caned nearly every day, was at last driven to stuffing his *Lederhosen* with newspapers, so that he could smile bravely under the flailing cane. When my grandfather discovered the trick, he was so enraged that poor Hugo was caned at home, as well as at school.

He was always the merry wanderer who yodels his way through a thousand traditional German songs. He was restless and irresponsible and prided himself on a devil-may-care attitude to life. He wanted to be a tragic actor. But the director of a Munich theatre shook his head and said, 'Can you imagine Hamlet with a Swabian burr? Why not try to become a good comedian – you have all the earmarks and your Swabian dialect is truly delightful.'

Hugo went home and cried on his mother's shoulder and became instead a dry goods clerk and a wine peddlar, as my Uncle Max told me later. He had quite a success travelling for his wine firm. As late as the 1960s his triumphal progressions through the villages of Swabia and the Black Forest were fondly remembered by the older men. Apparently he offered liberal tastings of his wares and naturally took the opportunity of checking up on them himself.

It had appealed to his spirit of adventure to enlist in 1914. Photographs show him as having exchanged his *Lederhosen*, Tyrolean hat and tankard of beer for field-grey and *Pickelhaube*, manning the field telephones. He eventually won the Iron Cross of which he was very proud. He survived the war physically intact, but suffered from shell-shock. I would observe with fascination how he would quite suddenly lose concentration and not hear a word of what was said to him. He would grind his teeth audibly with furious working of his jaws and wring his hands, till the veins stood out on them. His eyes bulged and became blood-shot and his expression became intense and fierce, quite unlike his usual genial grin. We children were told to pay no attention to his frightening transformation, which arose, we were assured, from the fact that Hugo had been a hero in the war. Indeed, his eyes would very quickly regain their normal expression as he relaxed and became his old self again. I don't think he was aware of these brief transformations.

At my grandfather's school there was a girl called Rosalie (all eighteen pupils from six to thirteen years were in one class) who was the first to inflame my father's susceptible heart. To show off to her he took up a dare to walk across the frozen village pond, although the children had been warned that it was not safe for skating. As he advanced to the middle, there was a loud, singing crack and a moment later the ice gave way and he disappeared in the inky water. My father claimed that only the presence of mind of a passer-by, who lay down at the edge of the pond, reaching out for his grasping hands and gradually drawing him to the surface, had saved his life. But in the descent through the ice he had bitten through his tongue and, dripping wet and streaming with blood, he had to be taken to the nearest town to have stitches put in. I recall the outrage we felt when he related how, after he had sufficiently recovered, he got a beating for his disobedience. When the story was told, we always clamoured to inspect his tongue, which, to our horrified delight displayed a scar all the way up and had one lobe extending a fraction beyond the other.

There is a story about Max which sounds rather Dickensian. He was a good-looking boy with fair curls. One day, so the story goes, a childless American couple was visiting the district and while driving through the village in their carriage, they saw Max. They asked him for directions and he obliged them politely, showing them the way. They were very taken with him and asked him his name, where he lived and who his parents were. Later they called upon my grandparents and asked if they might adopt Max and take him back to America. He would have far better chances if he returned with them, than if he remained in this small backwater of a village. Besides, with so many children, surely his parents could spare one? It was such an extraordinary request, and of course, my grandparents explained that because they had several children, it did not mean that they could spare one, or loved any of them the less. The couple had to return without Max.

The irony of this story is that when Max was seventeen he did go off to the New World to try his fortune. He contacted the couple in passing through New York and was kindly received. But it was only a visit; he successfully made his own way in America, remaining there for the rest of his life. He had been trained as an expert in the silk trade – judging quality and flaws – but being impatient at slow advancement, he left it and tried many things, including five years with the American government: the US Internal Revenue and Secret Service Department in Chicago. It was an easy job and gave him time to get married and to study lithography. Finally he took a post with the United States Printing and Lithography Company in Florida. He married a gentile girl from Baltimore, Lily, whom he worshipped. One year he took her to Germany to meet his father and the rest of the family. Unfortunately she too contracted tuberculosis and died before they were able to have any children. He never married again. He was never very wealthy, but had sufficient for his needs and happiness, although Lotte and I always called him 'our rich uncle in America' for on his flying visits to us, he always brought us treasures that seemed to come from Aladdin's cave. I particularly remember a solid gold arm-band with a clasp (which must have been his wife's) and I was heartbroken when I lost it. Almost as impressive were the glossy, brilliantly coloured labels, showing palm trees and blue seas, golden pineapples, glowing oranges in dark foliage from his lithographic company, which he never forgot to bring or send, knowing how much they pleased us. He was very fond of children and always regretted having none of his own. He wrote and illustrated several children's stories.

During my father's latter years at school he walked twice a week, seven kilometres each way, to the nearest market town of Horb to attend classes in English and French. He would have liked to have become a teacher like his father, but there was not enough money to pay for his training. He had, however, been lucky in his general education because Lehrer Zürndorfer, his father, appears to have taught a very generously conceived version of the Three Rs. An inspector's report on the school, dated 1879 lists the following subjects: religious instruction; reading; narration from memory; elocution; German language; handwriting; comprehension; written compositions; tabular analysis; local geography; history; punctuation; mental arithmetic; written arithmetic; geometry; drawing; exact sciences; singing; Latin for the top year and needlework for the girls provided by a visiting teacher.

So, at thirteen, emotionally still a child, still in need of his mother's care and affection, he left school and was sent to Rottweil in the Black Forest to be apprenticed to a firm of book-printers. As apprentice my father lived with the family, as was customary in those days, and got his board and lodging and some pocket-money while learning the trade. In his spare time he became a child again and joined in the games with the two children of the house who were much the same age. He told us that he enjoyed playing with us so much because 'I never did enough playing as a child'.

One detail of his early training fascinated us children. My father had very large ears with long lobes. The reason for his, he assured us, was that one of his daily duties had been to close the shutters of the workrooms last thing at night. This he sometimes forgot. When that happened, his master would pull him out of bed by the ear, and, still holding on to that convenient handle, would drag him down the stairs half-asleep and point out his omission. When we started commiserating indignantly with my father, he laughed and assured us that Herr Rosenstiel had been a good master and had taught him his business well. He stayed with the firm for several years, rising from apprentice to quite a senior position and remaining firm friends with the family until the old people died in 1932.

At seventeen he went to Strasbourg to become correspondent and first bookkeeper to the silk business of M. Wachenheimer, where he soon started enjoying the confidence of his bosses. He stayed with this firm for eleven years. It was during that time in this beautiful city that he continued his self-education. He took French lessons and attended a business school in the evenings. He read everything he could lay his hands on, and went to the theatre and opera as often as he could and started writing theatre reviews for the papers. His pieces were well received and eventually he became the regular critic on the *Frankfurter Zeitung* and the *Hamburger Blatt* and was on friendly terms with most of the actors and singers.

It was in Strasbourg that he met and fell in love with Klara whom he married in 1901 when he was twenty-eight. After his marriage he moved to Düsseldorf, but he always remembered those days affectionately and used to sing:

Oh Strassburg, oh Strassburg,
Du schöne alte Stadt

a song about the fine old city of Strasbourg, famous for its pretty girls, some of whom he had pursued as a stage-struck youth, throwing violets and verses at their feet.

3 Childhood

Shortly after the move to Gerresheim I caught the measles. I must have had it quite badly because I was sent to a children's hospital, a private one that had been highly recommended. My first few days there were traumatic. I had a high temperature and was delirious. The isolation cubicle had a glass partition, and the daily visits of my parents, who could only smile and wave and nod through the glass, were upsetting to everyone. I couldn't understand why my mother didn't come inside to talk to me and hold me, and she could only see me screaming at her, raging and streaming with tears. In the end my parents took to visiting me only at night, when they could reassure themselves with the sight of me asleep.

When the first stage was over, I was put with the other girls and boys in a long dormitory. One wall was entirely of glass and looked out on to lawns and gardens. It was winter and bitterly cold, but at night the glass partition was rolled back and the dormitory became a roofed veranda. It was wonderful. The stars seemed very close; the night was inside with us, and the snow glinted on the lawns, while we lay snugly in our blankets with the frosty air fresh on our faces.

During the day, if the sun was shining, our beds were wheeled out for a few hours on to the true veranda, protected only by a glass roof. I am astonished that my parents, who regarded draughts as lethal, could ever have been persuaded to send me to a place with such advanced ideas. It was in marked contrast with home where bath-nights were always an elaborate exercise in coddling. First the bathroom had to be correctly warmed, then we were soaped and washed by Mummy, and after being left to play a few bath-games, she and Daddy would each stand with a warmed towel to receive us as we dashed out of the bath. As soon as we were thoroughly dry we were put into our warmed nighties and dressing-gowns and rushed off to bed.

The rosy cheeks and healthy appetites of the convalescents lying out in the winter sunshine must have suggested to my shocked parents that children were hardier plants than they supposed. I was much happier once I was in the dormitory: I was well on the way to recovery and, besides, there were other children. One boy, a little older than the rest, thrilled me with his daring exploits. He would get out of bed when the nurses' backs were turned, and in his pyjamas do cartwheels all down the line of beds, or leap from bed to bed growling like a tiger. We little ones loved it.

'He was awfully naughty,' I confided to my mother later and she was satisfactorily horrified.

'He could have caught his death of cold!'

Now I was able to appreciate the toys which my parents, relatives and friends had sent in: games, books, crayons and drawing books, cut-out dolls with elaborate wardrobes, wooden farm animals and a magical box from my aunt Rosa from Ohligs with the much loved ribbons and trimmings, which were the envy of all the little girls in the dormitory.

I remember one day a nurse coming to my bed, admiring my many toys and asking if I could spare this or that for one or two children who had very little. But I was a selfish child, as my father never tired of telling me, and I acquiesced rather grudgingly, particularly when she took my sample-book of trimmings, uncomfortably aware that my father would not have been pleased with me.

I began to enjoy life in hospital. The food was good and imaginative. I looked forward particularly to three o'clock, when a glass of milk and a pretty little glass bowl with biscuits and a few sweets wrapped in coloured foil were provided for each child. At home I had been faddy, but here I ate everything avidly. None of the children had the washed-out faces of convalescents.

Evidently we all benefited from the drastic fresh-air cure, which in 1931 was an innovation.

Visiting days were now great fun. Parents and friends still had to keep their distance, but we could shout from our veranda to where they stood behind a barrier about twenty yards away. One day my parents brought my Aunt Rosa with them, and perhaps because of the lovely parcel of trimmings she had sent me, I felt I had to make a special effort at sociability; I suddenly stood up in bed, turned my back on the assembled company, lifted up my nightie and wiggled my bottom at them in the friendliest manner. I was quite nonplussed at the embarrassed silence that greeted this amiable gesture.

I didn't want to go home. I had got used to the daily routine of being with other children, of sleeping under the stars with the snow crunching under the feet of the night nurses and friendly doctors. Above all, I was sorry to leave behind all those wonderful toys which might otherwise have carried infection outside.

Measles had left me with a paralysed muscle in the right eye, giving me a squint. The specialists, who had never come aross anything like it before, presented me as an 'exhibit' at lectures in the teaching hospital. It quite pleased me to be the centre of attention, but my parents were very concerned. The doctors decided to do nothing for two years, since the eye might correct itself by then, which it did, to my parents' great relief.

I also rather enjoyed illnesses at home, though, no doubt, it is the convalescences that I remember. I enjoyed being fussed and indulged – Mummy read to me, neighbours visited me, Daddy told stories of his childhood and my appetite was tempted with my favourite dishes: fragrant ham, tomatoes, grapes. I used to enjoy lying in bed, just day-dreaming, or listening to the household sounds: milk bottles clinking, dishes being stacked, and to feel that everything was going on about me in a good regulated manner, while I lay comfortably in bed, watching the sun play in the curtains.

My mother was a great taker of temperatures and anything above 39° centigrade meant the doctor would be called in. Our doctor, Dr Lehmann, was a Jewish paediatrician who had looked after us since we were babies. Since we had got used to him and Mummy trusted him, he attended us in Gerresheim too, to begin with. 'Uncle Doctor' we used to call him and loved it when this dark, dapper little man sat down on our beds, cracking jokes with us, or letting us play with his stethoscope. He wore large, black-rimmed spectacles and had twinkling eyes and teeth. I was always intrigued by his hairy hands that seemed like small furry animals. But it was too expensive to call on Dr Lehmann from the centre of town for every minor ailment and so we started going to a local doctor, Dr Paulson, a mountain of a man, in appearance very like Charles Laughton. Dr Paulson was, in fact, an excellent doctor, rather bluff and business-like, without Dr Lehmann's polish, but with qualities that we were to appreciate later.

When I was seven my parents thought I would benefit from some sun and sea air, though they were not able to get away themselves. They decided to send me to a *Ferienheim*. Holiday homes had become quite popular in Germany. They were usually private ventures: someone would take a large house by the sea or in the mountains, engage qualified staff and take a limited number of children, carefully arranged into age groups, away on holiday.

I was sent to Zingst on the North Sea for six weeks. I didn't want to go and kicked up rather a fuss, but in the event I enjoyed it. I had never seen the sea. In Germany the sea is not familiar as it is in Britain. To me it was a mysterious, remote entity heard of in stories of shipwrecks or sea-nymphs. The real thing exceeded my expectations: long stretches of silver sand, everlasting sunshine and this blue, glistening being that stretched and heaved and curled on the beach and sighed continually.

A few vignettes of this holiday remain in my mind. There was the daily procession, two by two, to the beach. I hated that, but loved the long, timeless morning on the beach that followed; the joys of sand and water, of feeling hot, with a salty taste on one's lips. At noon a whistle was blown and we all sat down in a large circle in the sand. To my daily delight a group of maids arrived with two large cane clothes-baskets, one filled to the brim with shiny red tomatoes, the other containing sandwiches. I recall the sensuous delight of seeing the tomatoes in such glossy abundance, anticipating the first bite into the smooth skin. We were all hungry and enjoyed these beach picnics enormously. We little ones had to rest a while during the heat of midday under large, brightly coloured beach umbrellas. In the late afternoon came the walk back to the house with a softer sun and longer shadows and the exciting smell of wood-smoke on the air.

One incident at Zingst made a deep impression on me. We had been divided into two age groups: the under-elevens and the teenagers. The 'big' boys and girls seemed to be leading their own lives on the beach, swimming, playing ball-games, and the only time we had any real contact with them was at picnic time, when there was a general roll-call.

One day I was watching some big boys digging a large hole in the sand and a girl lying down in it. Amid laughter and jokes they covered her up, bit by bit, till she had completely disappeared from sight. They went on playing and I lost interest. When the whistle blew for lunch it was discovered that the girl was missing, and in some agitation the boys explained that they could not find the spot where they had buried her, although they had been looking ever since. There were no landmarks in the sand; it lay there as inscrutable as the sea itself.

The whole place was suddenly turned into a frantic anthill: everyone started digging and scraping. The organizer and most of the staff had been sent for, and even the police, and the search was systematically conducted under their directions. After what seemed like hours, the girl was at last unearthed, unconscious. I thought she was dead. Artificial respiration was administered and at last her eyelashes flickered, and, pale and sandy, she was carried away. On this occasion we missed our lunch; one boy was sent home in disgrace and for the rest of the holiday surveillance was much stricter. I have always remembered the shared feeling of suspense and terror during the search.

Then suddenly the days by the sea were over and it was time to go home. As the train ran into Düsseldorf Station I caught sight of the familiar figure of my father, eagerly running towards our compartment. I remember the conflicting feelings of embarrassment and sheer relief at seeing him again after such a long time. I felt that I had come from a different world and could not at once reconcile the two.

By then I had been at school for a year. My first day at school had been quite an occasion. My father, who loved making ceremonies out of quite ordinary happenings, handed over to me with due pomp before the assembled family an enormous *Schultüte* (a paper cornet, almost as tall as I was) full to the brim with chocolates and sweets. I had a large new leather satchel, to be worn on the back, a red dress in the distinctive *Bleyle* style and a white embroidered apron, and my two front teeth missing. And so, on the first day of the Easter term 1932, Mummy took me to the school and delivered me into the classroom. Of course, I cried as soon as Mummy left and, among all the other weeping children, I persisted longest. I simply would not stop. The teacher, Fräulein Rätchen, with sandy hair and pale blue eyes behind pink-rimmed spectacles, noticed and called me out to her. She knelt down by me and asked me my name.

'Hannele Zürndorfer,' I sobbed.

She took my hands and said, 'Hannele? Why, you've got the same name as I have.'

'Are you called Hannele too?' I asked, shaken out of my sorrow by surprise.

'I am called Hanna, and Hannele means little Hanna.'

This put an end to my weeping: that a teacher should have the same name as me! I always felt that this was a bond between us. I must have settled into school quite quickly, because I do not remember any particularly unhappy occasions. Everybody went to the *Volksschule* (primary school), where boys and girls were in separate classes from the start. I enjoyed being together with the other children and made many friends.

School started at eight and finished around two; during the first year we finished at twelve or one. We had a mid-morning luncheon break and some homework, which in those early years did not take very long. The school was only about five minutes' walk away with only one road to cross, so that very soon I went there by myself.

It was Daddy who used to get us our breakfasts of porridge with raisins and nuts and a cup of chocolate. Then, (for I always dawdled till the last moment) he would stand at the window while I was careering past, and holding up his pocket-watch on a chain, he would point at it to show that I had still five minutes to spare. He always put his watch fast, for he knew my weakness. I am not sure that this system was sound. I still dawdle but now find that most clocks are right.

Arithmetic was my weak point. My father, like many people who have to deal with practical business early in life, was good at figures and often astounded us with feats of mental calculation. Often he tried to help me when I could not do my sums. Though a patient man, these sessions became so distressing to both of us that after a while he abandoned them. He simply could not understand my inability to grasp what seemed to him quite obvious points.

'A daughter of mine and unable to do such simple sums!' Then I would start crying and be unable to do anything at all, so that both of us ended up shouting, I soggy with tears, till in the end my book was hurled across the floor, with me none the wiser.

One shameful incident connected with school I remember well because of my father's awesome reactions. He laid great stress on honesty and truthfulness. In his estimation, to lie was probably the most terrible thing, with ingratitude coming a close second. One day we had an arithmetic test in class and I got every single answer wrong. Fräulein Rätchen read out the answers and we had to tick or cross them ourselves. Some wicked impulse drove me to rub out two of my wrong answers and insert the correct ones. Fräulein Rätchen's eagle eye caught me writing.

'Were you tampering with your answers?' she asked me sternly. Shamefacedly I admitted that I was. She called me out to her desk and the extravagant reactions of the usually so gentle teacher quite surprised me.

'*You!* You of all people! *You cheating!*' and she soundly boxed my ear. I felt terribly upset. How was I going to break the news to my father? He always enquired how tests had gone and I saw no way of keeping my disgrace from him. Whenever I had some unpleasant news to impart I would consult with my mother first, or even beg her to break it to him gently. Her concept of integrity was not quite as strict as my father's. But on this occasion she refused me any comfort and said I must tell Daddy myself. Accordingly, after dinner, when Daddy asked me how the test had gone, I falteringly confessed. His reaction was not violent, as I had feared, but worse. He looked at me long with his calm grey eyes and said very quietly, '*You*, a daughter of *mine*, to lie and cheat. I will have nothing to do with you.' And for two days he would not speak to me.

During the first few terms at school we used slates, with slate-pencils, covered halfway down with coloured paper to hold them by. Those with shiny papers in red or blue with little stars on them were more expensive than the others. We had to keep the pencils sharp and Daddy was expert at getting them to a fine point with his knife. These we carried in a pencil box, and we each had to crochet a couple of cloths to wipe our slates after cleaning them with pink rubber sponges. The sponges had to be rinsed and moistened every day at home. So the procedure with slates, sticks and sponges was really quite complicated, even intriguing, and all the equipment was the subject of a daily inspection by the teacher. It used to please me to see the rows of boxes set out on our desks in all their variety: there were plain wooden ones, polished ones and others with painted pictures or carved patterns. The most desirable ones were in black lacquer with silver squiggly lines incised on them and a little sponge-box to match. Then there was the thrill of transferring to paper and pencil, and later still to ink, with pen-holder, nib, nib-cloth and blotting-paper in all the colours of the rainbow.

When my sister started school she used to have her nightly *Koller* (tantrums). She would become hysterically obsessed with having everything ready for next day before she went to bed. Then she would get out of bed several times to make quite sure that her sponge was moist enough, her slate-pencils sharp enough and her slate-cloth clean, and would it be dry by morning? As she got older this developed into a strong, competitive spirit: she would slave away before tests and unless she was top she would moan and weep and work harder than ever. I was far more easy-going and quite happy to cruise along, except in composition. I thoroughly enjoyed that: was I not my father's daughter, born on the hundredth anniversary of Marlitt's birth?

During my first four years at school Fräulein Rätchen was my only teacher, except for gym once a week, and needlework. This latter subject was taught by Fräulein Rätchen's elder sister; they lived together, both spinsters. My needlework was as bad as my arithmetic. I was not very neat or tidy and my little rag, purporting to be a pot-holder, was held up in class with an air of disgust, as an example of how not to do it. However, I soon became sufficiently proficient at crocheting egg-cosies so that I showered all my relatives with these for birthdays, Easter and Christmas.

My class was quite a large one; there were about fifty of us. My special friend was a girl called Ella Hertneck. Though my age, she was far more robust and much taller than me. She had brown plaits and lived a few doors away with her mother and grandfather. They were jolly, unconventional people. The mother, a big, red-cheeked widow, was a friendly, blunt woman, working part-time to help keep the family. The house was usually rather untidy, but one was always welcome.

Ella and I were 'best friends', playing with our dolls, roller-skating, tobogganing and joining in the many street games that were popular at that time. The residential streets were then a playground for children; there were few cars, tradesmen delivered by horse and cart and sweepers used to come along daily with their shovels and buckets on wheels.

One of the most popular games which was played by the older children with great vigour was *Völkerball*, a type of hand-ball game with two teams and complicated rules. It was a great day when the older children allowed us to take part. Games seemed to go with seasons. There was the hopscotch season with its chalked pavements and quaint rhymes, which might be followed by a craze for spinning tops or whipping hoops. The brightly painted wooden tops were of enormous variety and quite a lot of skill was required to twist the string correctly round the spindle and then twitch the stick to get the top spinning. Then, with luck, one could whip it all down the road, leaping and dancing along. The wooden hoops too hurtled along, kept carefully in control by the whipping-stick. Woe to the pedestrian who got in the way! Marbles was another favourite. We used to work a hollow into the earth round the trees. The marbles had to be flicked into the hole and if you knocked one of your opponent's marbles out into the road, you could take it. The last marble in the hole took all the rest. They were clay marbles in lovely earth colours of red, green, brown, and blue, so we knew our own. Five clay marbles were worth one gorgeous glass marble with twisted colours running through. This was not used for playing, but as a repository of value. We each had a little marble-bag. Sometimes we set out with a heavy bag and came home with it empty, or vice versa. Of course, there was also hide-and-seek, catching games, skipping and ball-games played against a straight wall.

As ours was a corner house with several steps leading from the street to the front door, it became a favourite spot for children to meet to sit and talk. Sometimes we would be roused by the appearance of the barrel-organ man and we would rush indoors to beg money for the threadbare monkey dressed in frills and silk. They were good times and I felt part of the street community. Naturally there were feuds, or fights between girls and boys. Many a day I would come home with bleeding knees after a roller-skating skirmish, but it was all in good sport. I still had a couple of years before I became aware of personal animosity towards me, or was made to feel different or an outsider because I was Jewish.

Winter in Gerresheim was a particularly happy time. We had at least five or six weeks of snow every winter, and it was marvellous snow: thick and clean with blue shadows in the sunlight. I loved to watch the first snow falling: large grey flakes from behind the window-pane, settling soundlessly on branches, fences and streetlamps. I loved the sense of warmth and safety it engendered. Then came the first snowman, the first snowball, and suddenly winter, lovely white, Christmassy, lamplit winter had begun!

Snowball-fights raged up and down the street and even grown-ups sometimes became involved. Snowmen nodded at each other from the front gardens with their hats and black noses, and as soon as school was out, we would be off with our toboggans to a hilly wood not far away. Daddy had bought us a large toboggan with metal runs and we used to be up and down the hills all afternoon long until the lamps were lit. For these occasions Mummy had bought us track-suits, such as are worn for jogging today. One year a boy whizzed straight into a tree and split open his head.

When I was still too small to go on my own with the other children, Mummy used to take Lotte and me into the woods. She was very skilful at steering the sledge down steep slopes, often between trees. She was quite intrepid. I think she enjoyed it as much as we did and on the way home she gave us turns on the sledge.

In these matters my mother was far more daring than my father. She was a good oars-woman too, and whenever the opportunity offered she would take us out onto the lake for a row. My father would never join us, but fluttered anxiously round the lake like a mother hen, exhorting Mummy to take care. She would laugh gaily and scold him for being an old worry-guts. I loved her in these carefree moods.

In her youth she had been madly fond of dancing; she was proud of her shapely legs and in frivolous moods she would lift her skirt a little above the knee and whirl around the room. To her sorrow my father was no good at dancing. When Uncle Hugo came to stay he and my mother used to dance the *Schuhplattler* (a Bavarian folk dance) together. They would career wildly round, with Hugo gleefully smacking his heels and the seat of his trousers with his palms, until my mother had to sit down panting, with her soft brown eyes alive and sparkling.

We still had a living-in maid in those days. Änne had come to Gerresheim with us from our old house. I remember her only dimly, but I am told that I was very fond of her, as she had been with me ever since I was a toddler. When she left to get married, there was a procession of maids of whom I remember nothing, except that I resented them for not being Änne. Our last living-in maid I do recall well, Anna Hiehstand, a young Catholic girl from the Black Forest, large and good-natured, who tried her best with me and whom, I am told, I plagued bitterly for quite a time. She had dark plaits reaching down to her waist. Although I was often rude and unmannerly, I think I must have liked her more than the others, because I still remember how I enjoyed my occasional visits to the Catholic church with her on Sunday mornings. Anna asked if I might accompany her and my father made no objection. Though steadfastly Jewish, he was very broadminded and respected other religions. In fact, once he said to me that the most beautiful prayer he knew was the Lord's Prayer.

I used to come back from church enraptured. I still recall my delight at the light rioting through the stained glass windows and I think I responded to the solemn, devout atmosphere and the singing that filled the vaulted roof. I found no such solemn atmosphere in my rare visits to the synagogue, because on the women's side, where we had to sit, there was continual chatter. I was very sorry when Anna Hiehstand had to leave us later around 1935 or '36 and felt guiltily that it was my fault for having been horrid to her. It wasn't. She left because it was by then no longer healthy for an 'Aryan' girl to be seen working for a Jew.

4 Festivals

Although my father was wholeheartedly Jewish, we kept Christmas as well as Channukah, and Easter as well as Passover. The official excuse was that we could not deprive our Catholic maids of their festivals, but I suspect that my father, who always got the most out of ceremonial occasions, thoroughly enjoyed the Christian feasts, especially Christmas. He loved giving presents and surprises, and this was the opportunity *par excellence*. Besides, through his many Christian friends, who showered Lotte and me with presents, he found himself drawn into the feast willy-nilly.

For all indulged children Christmas must be marvellously exciting, and so it was for us. Mystery was the keynote: closed doors, rustling paper and the sharp smell of pine. Lotte, Anna, the maid, and I stood waiting with suppressed excitement until there sounded the most silvery of bells and the doors of the darkened room opened slowly. I was aware only of a magic glow at the far end. There the tall, dark green spruce stood transformed. It was set with a trembling mantle of white candles; glistening strands of silver hair flowed over the branches and the top was crowned with a large silver star. There were no glass balls or other ornaments. It was the simplicity of soft candlelight flickering in the silver filaments and trembling over the polished pine-needles that I found so beautiful. Somehow this soft effulgence became identified with a bursting feeling of love for my parents, hovering benignly in the shadows.

Then we all sang carols, 'Oh Tannenbaum', 'Silent Night' and others, my mother and I always slightly out of tune. And all the time the presents lay heaped beneath the tree in shadowy mystery. Although I was dying to undo the carefully wrapped parcels, I was always reluctant to start, to break this breathless spell. But once I had started, I was like one possessed, utterly oblivious of my surroundings, tearing off wrapper after wrapper, gilded string and shiny bow, and drawing forth books and paints, dolls and games and toys in what seemed a never-ending variety. Wish after wish was fulfilled. There were kind remembrances from Oma and Opa, from aunts and uncles, cousins and great-aunts, friends and acquaintances. Gradually a lassitude would steal over me. I was overwhelmed, I did not want any more, although there were still presents unopened. I would perhaps retreat into the corner with one small object and start playing, leaving the other things untouched. Then I would start un-wrapping again, until everything was gone and I felt regret that there was nothing more to undo. I would glance across at Lotte's things, comparing, evaluating. Perhaps there would be some particularly large object, such as a scooter, or a dolls' pram, or a large new doll complete with wardrobe, roller-skates, or ice-skates, a grocer's shop, or a post office, or new clothes.

I thanked my parents elaborately, hugging and kissing them, and the time of goodwill was upon us indeed. After the first thrill was over and everything had been admired, examined and compared, I always wanted to go out into the street with some of my new treasures for the world to admire. Other children had the same idea. I would meet them airing new dolls and strutting in new clothes, or barking their knees on new roller-skates and ringing the bells of wobbling new bicycles. Lotte would be trudging beside me struggling with a huge doll that bleated 'maa-maa' at every step, while I fussed over a shiny new pram with an adjustable hood and blue satin eiderdown. Then it was time to go home to a starched damask tablecloth, glasses sparkling with wine, chicken and rice, and everybody kind – nobody cross about anything.

Channukah, the Jewish feast of the eight candles, was quite different. There too was the glow of candlelight, there too were gifts, but it seemed a more serious occasion. For me it lacked mystery and the pagan quality that came with the tree brought in from the dark forests. But my father made it a poignant and significant occasion, particularly in the later days of persecution.

The old brass candelabrum, the *Menorah*, that had been passed down through several generations, was brought out and polished till it shone. It had eight main arms and a small ninth arm in front for the 'servant' candle, from which the others had to be lit, one candle more each night. On the eighth night all nine candles, the 'servant' candle too, were burning and their light seemed to grow and suffuse the whole room. We sang '*Mohauzur jeshuezee . . .*' my mother always tripping over the hissing consonants and my father's eyes aglow with that look that always made me want to melt with tenderness. There would be a little gift for each of us and a festive meal. Then Daddy would tell us the story of Channukah; about the drop of oil that kept the Holy Temple lamp burning for eight days while the brave Macabees defied the besieging army. Afterwards we all played family games together and Daddy read to us. One of our favourites was the highly romantic tale of 'Rosa von Tannenburg'. Rosa's nobly-born father was imprisoned by wicked barons, but Rosa's steadfastness and love withstood the most harrowing of trials and foiled the barons' dastardly schemes. Ultimately, justice was done and there were tears in all our eyes. At other times he recited Schiller and Goethe to us: 'The Erl-King's Daughter', 'The Diver' and 'The Sorcerer's Apprentice', which was a great favourite of mine, because my father used to enhance the climax of the poem by a dramatic pause while the house flooded and the apprentice tried in vain to undo the spell.

Before either Channukah or Christmas came my birthday on 5 December. It coincided with the Feast of St Nicholas, when we were given nuts and apples and gingerbread men at school and sang Christmas carols. But as it was also my birthday, I had to stand in front of the class to be wished 'Happy Birthday' by the children. Fräulein Rätchen had made it a custom for the birthday child to select a song, a sweet and a picture-card from her stock of flower fairies, each with a little verse underneath, and also a coloured hair-ribbon. At home there would be presents and the meal of my choice: boiled beef, sauté potatoes and a variety of salads. In the afternoon children came for tea, some with their parents. For every child Daddy would buy a chocolate-covered pastry ball filled with fresh cream, known as *Mohrenkopf* (Moor's head), from the *Konditorei* in the Königsallee. There would also be a plate of marzipan apples, pears, or pigs. Apart from that there were the usual cakes and biscuits and sandwiches and in the midst of everything the birthday-wreath, with a candle for each year and one extra, the *Lebenslicht*.

December was for me always the happiest of months and no wonder January came as an anticlimax. But in February was *Fasching*. *Fasching* in Düsseldorf was a rollicking occasion when for several days the Rhinelanders forgot their cares in revelry. Hock, Moselle and beer were consumed in great quantities. It was mainly a time for the grown-ups, with carousing and fancy-dress balls that lasted till morning.

The high point of the whole occasion was the grand *Fasching* parade through the main streets. Some children took part, the rest went to watch. But whether or not you actually walked in the parade, you wore fancy dress and your attendant grown-ups at least sported a funny hat or mask. Everyone carried rattles and threw streamers and blew through those things that unrolled and squeaked and fluttered a feather at the end. There were crackers, bouquets of balloons, fireworks and blizzards of confetti.

For us the excitement started well before we left the house. I remember I was once dressed as a little Dutch girl, gauze-hat, fichu, clogs and all, and Lotte was Little Red Riding Hood in bonnet and skirt of red velvet, with her skinny legs in their white stockings protruding like matchsticks. Anna Hiehstand came dressed in her Black Forest costume, with her dark hair carefully braided under an elaborate black head-dress.

We were lucky that one of Daddy's colleagues at work lived in the main street in a house with a balcony, so we could watch from there. We went by taxi, on tenterhooks for fear we should never get through the crowds. At last we reached the grandstand. The crush of people was so dense that it seemed we would surely have been trodden underfoot, had we been in the street below. Soon we felt the throb of the first brass band, and then they came – the decorated floats representing all the leading firms of the town. One of the wine companies had excelled itself: nearly naked girls, grinning bravely in the cold February air, nestled among purple balloons that had been joined together to form clusters of giant grapes wreathed in silken foliage. At the other end Dionysius rolled with his companions among garlanded barrels, drinking Hock from enormous goblets. Other floats represented fairy tales or nursery rhymes: Sleeping Beauty in a bower of crêpe roses and Lucky Hans with live piglets squealing and staggering and geese honking and flapping their wings.

In between the floats cavorted groups of people in grotesque masks. There were gipsies with tambourines, long-haired troubadours, tramps clowning all the way, street urchins turning cartwheels (a specialty of Düsseldorf) and decorated hand-carts. The civic authorities marched past trying to maintain their dignity, followed by various clubs and associations, each in its distinctive uniform. There was a section of children too, many of whom looked rather cold and blue in their thin costumes; the wise ones were disguised as wolves or bears. There was an equestrian section with dashing hussars whose horses snorted and shied whenever there were any hold-ups and frequently spoiled the effect by dropping steaming turds on the road. Marches and traditional songs, carefully interspersed, were played continuously by the bands. Batons were twirled and thrown, drums boomed, flags furled and unfurled and confetti rained down from the windows and balconies on to the squealing crowds below. We too emptied our bags of confetti and blew our streamers into the air.

When *Fasching* was over and the streets had been swept clean everything seemed stale for a while, but for many a night I recalled the bright succession of floats before I went to sleep.

There was no other public festival until the feast of St Martin in autumn. We children used to gather at school, warmly clad, each carrying a paper lantern on a long stick. When the band arrived we formed into a long column, about four abreast. Then the ghostly glittering serpent wound its way through Gerresheim, led by the mounted figure of St Martin in a wide cloak. At a certain point the procession halted, while St Martin re-enacted the old legend by taking off his cloak and giving it to the beggar who lay patiently waiting.

The lanterns were usually round, brilliant red, orange or yellow, but some children carried much-coveted lanterns in the shape of animal-heads, moons, stars or suns, or intricately patterned ones. I felt spellbound as we moved slowly like a glowing centipede through the night. The stars, by comparison, seemed cold and far away. On either side of the procession, every few yards, a shadowy grown-up moved like a ghost. As the file of lanterns bobbed and swayed through the darkness, older boys and girls sometimes fooled about and set their lanterns on fire. That was exciting too. We had been drilled to cast our flaming lantern down while one of the grown-ups would hasten to stamp it out. Of course, those behind had to wait until the emergency was over. As we moved, glowing links in a long, winding chain, we sang the St Martin's song. At the dispersal point I was collected by my parents, a minute glow-worm, drugged with wonder and half-asleep.

Pesach, or Passover, was a Jewish family feast that I thoroughly enjoyed. It commemorated the exodus of the Jews from Egypt and the larger the family gathering, the easier I found it to imagine that we really were the descendants of the twelve tribes. My father thrived in his role of patriarch, and the arrival of relatives from various parts of Germany made it an exuberant and sometimes noisy occasion.

The Passover I remember best was the last really large gathering, before relations started emigrating. There were about seventeen or twenty of us around the table, which had been extended to its utmost with an extra table set across the end. There was the best china and silver, stiffly starched napkins and tablecloth and beautiful, cut crystal wine glasses in sparkling colours. By the side of my father stood a huge platter containing ten little dishes for the bitter herbs, spices and condiments, the harsh or bitter taste of each representing one of the ten plagues. The only ones I can recall are very hot, grated horseradish, finely chopped parsley, a paste of apple, almonds and wine, salt water and the shank bone of a lamb. In the middle of this stood a goblet of wine. Each person had a piece of matzoh (a kind of water biscuit), representing the unleavened bread of the first Passover. No crumb of ordinary bread was allowed in the house at Passover and tradition demanded a token search of the house, which my father conducted with customary gusto, on the previous day. Beside each plate was a copy of the *Hagadah*, an illustrated text of the Passover service. Done in full, it could last as long as four hours, while people got hungrier and hungrier, but my father conducted a shortened version, lasting about an hour and a half. Naturally he concentrated on the more spectacular passages. The part I remember best is the rehearsal of the Ten Plagues, each of which was pictured in the *Hagadah* by rather naive drawings, reminiscent of the illustrations of *Struwelpeter*. The ritual consisted of dipping our matzoh into each of the ten dishes in turn, taking a nibble, then dipping a finger into our wine glasses and vigorously shaking off the drop of wine, whilst vehemently enunciating the Hebrew name of the plague represented. It was marvellously spine-chilling as we boomed in unison: *'dom'* (blood), *'vorad'* *(hail)*, *'kinim'* (vermin), and so on, through boils, darkness, locusts and other unpleasantnesses, until finally, with fearful solemnity we thundered *'Macchus!'* (death of the firstborn). This was the last straw at which even the Egyptians had enough. I could never quite understand why they were so obtuse in learning their lesson.

Then came the meal of roast meats that the Israelites had eaten before setting out. We usually had a joint of venison to represent the roast kid of the original Passover.

There were parts of the ritual that particularly involved children and to these Lotte and I always looked forward. Beside my father, hidden under a white napkin, lay a piece of matzoh preserved from the previous year which we had to 'steal' without my father noticing. We had to hide it away so well that he could not find it, and in this we could count on the help of conspiring relatives. When my father confessed himself defeated and we triumphantly produced the matzoh, he would reward us with nuts and raisins.

A special role was allocated to the youngest member of the family; in our case that was Lotte. But until she was old enough I was allowed to 'question' my father on the significance of the Passover feast. The child has to step up to the head of the table and recite in Hebrew, *'Manistano haleiloh haseh . . .'* ('How does this night differ from other nights?') and through question and answer, the father explains it all. Grudgingly I handed over this important task for Lotte to perform, when she was four, under the eyes of adoring relatives.

All through the long service and festive meal I felt occasional thrills of anticipation for there was one empty place at the table and a goblet of wine stood waiting. It was waiting for Elijah. Often I found myself glancing towards the door – deliberately left open – wondering whether this might not be the occasion, surely to come, when the prophet might decide to join us and drink his glass of wine. He never came, but I can never watch the ghost of Banquo occupying the empty seat at Macbeth's feast, without thinking of Elijah.

At any mention of Passover, I see our large silk lampshade of antique gold, with golden fringe, a little faded, and the silk almost transparent, with a large stain on one side. When I asked why the damaged shade had not been replaced, I was told that it was kept as a reminder to my father not to lose his temper.

Here was an object lesson on which he seized. Years ago there had been a Passover gathering, attended by the whole *Mischpoche*. Uncle Hugo's wife, Gretel, was known for her sharp tongue and her inability to resist malicious gossip and tale-telling, often the cause of family upsets. Poor Uncle Hugo had met her when he was recovering from shell-shock and she had been a nurse, a rather dominating one, I suspect. Passover was a time for harmony, but Gretel had arrived all set for mischief and continued throughout the service with sly digs and censorious references about some absent member of the family. Eventually my father lost his temper and, picking up the large soup tureen that had just been placed in front of him, he dashed it down on the table. The hot soup went everywhere, splashing the lampshade and even the ceiling, as well as the guests. I am not sure how that Passover feast ended, but my father never allowed himself to forget his loss of temper. But his moral tale misfired, for instead of being horrified, I was highly impressed and delighted by his reaction, for had not *Tante* Gretel, with her strident and condemnatory voice, often scolded me and got me deliberately into trouble? She was my least favourite aunt.

Purim and Sukkos are two other Jewish feasts. Purim was an occasion for fancy-dress performances by the children of the Jewish community before their admiring elders. Mummy used to make our costumes and rehearse us in our parts until we were word-perfect. Once I represented a comet, wearing yards of gathered tulle, studded with sequins and trailing behind me a silver lamé tail. Another time I wore *Lederhosen*, braces and a little Tyrolean hat, singing a couple of my father's Swabian folk songs with the appropriate gestures, but Lotte, aged four, recited 'Susannah in the Bath', wearing a long dressing-gown and carrying a huge sponge and stole the show with her solemn lisping.

Sukkos was the harvest festival, a pagan celebration of fruitfulness. A rough hut would be erected in the synagogue grounds, made of logs and leafy branches. Inside it was festooned with sheaves of corn, poppy-wreaths, creamy gourds and melons glowing like suns. There were baskets of apples and pears; bunches of grapes dropped from the roof and spears of maize flashed out of curling leaves. Everyone joined hands and danced in a circle around the hut.

One year my father built us our own little Sukkos hut in the woods, all of us helping to intertwine the branches to form a little bower. We decorated it with ears of corn and wild flowers and ate nuts and apples. This is the Sukkos I remember best. We left the little hut with its treasures to the birds and rabbits, or anyone else who might chance upon it.

Easter I liked almost as much as Christmas. On Easter Sunday I woke to the sound of bells and watched the spring sunshine stealing through the curtains, across the carpet, up the walls, over the ceiling to linger on the arms of the lamp. There, in their angle rested a huge Easter egg, wrapped in shiny blue foil-paper and tied with a large blue bow! On the toy-cupboard, in the arms of Susannah, Lotte's doll, was an identical egg in pink. At breakfast time, eyes eagerly straying around the room, we ate our brightly coloured boiled eggs, then scrambled down from the table, hurrying from room to room. We hunted out the little nests placed in woven baskets, in which squatted tiny chocolate Easter hares surrounded by eggs: sugar eggs, or chocolate ones wrapped in brightly patterned papers. We *were* indulged. One record Easter I remember counting twelve nests. The fascination was the hunt itself, rather than the eggs. And it continued on our Easter Sunday morning walk, following the trail of the Easter hare.

On this occasion my father's walking stick was endowed with a special power: if it danced on the ground twice, it meant the hare had passed that way, if it bounced three times it meant that the hare had actually dropped some of his precious burden close by. Our eyes were riveted to the walking stick; the impulse never seemed to come from my father's hand, but from the stick itself. There were frantic searchings in the dewy grass, in the boles of trees and in the twigs of bushes. There were whoops of delight as we pounced on a red gleam in a cluster of primroses to uncover an egg! Some eggs were dropped by my father surreptitiously while our attention was elsewhere – though I kept an eager eye on him – but the bulk of them (so I was told later) had been hidden the night before. The way led through twisty paths and thickets, and how he was able to remember exactly where he had put each egg is beyond my comprehension. Only once did the magic fail. Although the stick jumped three times and although my father joined in the search, egg we found none, and he seemed rather puzzled.

If it had rained during the night the eggs, which were wrapped, were unharmed. It was in fact all the more convincing to find eggs wet with raindrops in the sodden grass. There was the risk that other people might come before we did, but no one seems to have penetrated as deeply into the woods as we used to do.

This Easter morning outing was really only a special version of our regular Sunday morning walks. On a small scale, my father's beloved *Gerresheimer Schweiz* offered everything: hills, woods and meadows. When we went there we were not allowed to dawdle and if Lotte could not keep up she would be lifted on to his shoulders.

They were memorable walks. Depending on what we saw, my father told us about plants and birds, about forests that were pressed down thousands of years ago to become coal, about Neanderthal man; he talked about everything under the sun and we were a willingly captive audience.

We might come upon an old, abandoned boot. My father would poke it with the metal tip of his ever-present walking stick (his 'third leg') and start off with something like, 'That boot, if it could talk, could tell us some wonderful stories, I'm sure.'

We would look up expectantly and he would proceed to do just that. In the course of the tale we would pass from cowhide to factory and shop and travel through many lands, and then we would join in trying to suggest how it came to be lying here, now, without its fellow. It became a sort of game to try to invent stories about anything, which certainly helped to stimulate our imaginations and sometimes in later years came in very handy when writing school essays. But sometimes we just marched along singing, suddenly veering off to plunge downhill into the banks of fallen leaves. We picked wild strawberries, bilberries and blackberries, which we ate on the spot, as well as flowers to take home to Mummy.

There was a certain young tree with branches low enough for us to reach. It grew about half-way along our walk. We always anticipated it eagerly, because it was a 'magic' tree whose branches provided sandwiches just when we were beginning to feel hungry. As with the Easter eggs, I never managed to discover how my father hung the sandwiches there without our seeing. As I grew older I tried to catch him out, but never succeeded. We called the tree the *Lebkuchenbaum* (gingerbread tree), because the first time we came on it, it produced *Leipziger Lebkuchen*. It was extremely versatile.

We often wished Mummy could be with us on these walks and in later times I have sometimes thought how unfair it was to leave her behind to cook the Sunday dinner, but I think she preferred it. Often she did not feel well enough for such long walks. And all of us appreciated her efforts and looked forward eagerly to the meal. The Sunday dinner I enjoyed best was boiled chicken and bouillon rice with salad. We would regale her minutely with all our adventures and she always listened with interest.

After dinner and a little rest it was Mummy's turn. She changed her clothes and smartened us up for the family walk along the main shopping street of Gerresheim. Mummy would stop and linger here and there, gazing at a dress, or some shoes, or pots of flowers at the florist's. Gerresheim shop-windows were no Champs d'Elysée, or even a Königsallee. I don't know whether Mummy actually enjoyed those Sunday afternoons; they seemed a poor treat to me.

I *did* enjoy shopping with her in the Benderstrasse when the streets and shops were alive with people, particularly after school, on early winter evenings when the streetlamps and shop lights had been lit. My favourite shop was the delicatessen, kept by an oddly assorted couple. She was a tiny, dark bird of a woman with black eyes like a sparrow and he was a fair giant, slow and kind. Both of them smiled a great deal and took a lot of trouble. Nearly all my favourite foods came out of their barrels: pickled herrings, pickled gherkins and smoked eel.

Herr Portens, the baker, sold currant buns flavoured with cinnamon, for five Pfennig each. He also delivered crisp, white rolls every morning in time for breakfast. My favourite bread was a plaited loaf made of fine white wheat-flour with poppy seeds on top. Herr Portens didn't make those, but Daddy brought one home from town every Friday evening for Kiddush.

Kiddush is a ceremony to mark the beginning of Sabbath. My father kept it up as long as we were together as a family. He used to come home in good time from work and we were allowed to stay up a little later than usual. The table was spread with a clean white cloth. We usually had veal cutlet, sauté potatoes and salad, and Lotte and I were allowed a small glass of red wine that was an essential part of the cermony. The evening always ended with our parents' blessing. I used to like the solemnity of that. First my father, then my mother laid their hands upon our heads saying, 'May the Lord bless you and keep you; may the Lord make his face to shine upon you and give you peace.'

My father always said it in Hebrew, but my mother used to stammer and falter, till she gave it up as a bad job and spoke the blessing in German.

5 The Last Holiday

My memories of the early 1930s are of a happy time, when my parents seemed to have no concerns apart from our welfare. But things were changing imperceptibly. Probably the first hints for me were the gradual preoccupation of my father and the serious adult conversations that stopped suddenly at our approach. Two incidents, though unconnected with the political currents of those days, somehow for me mark the beginning of a time of insecurity and dimly perceived anxieties.

For our last family holiday in the summer of 1936, when I was nearly eleven, we stayed in a small Jewish guest house in Sieben Urlei, a village in the Moselle region. My mother had not been well and needed a holiday. It was lovely wooded country, the weather was perfect and we were having a wonderful time. Suddenly, after only a few days, my father was called away to the town of Eller to advise the widow of a colleague on a business problem. 'Eller' and 'Frau Gietzen' were names I knew well, for throughout my childhood my father, who was the late Herr Gietzen's trustee, had from time to time to make such visits. He thoroughly enjoyed them, for his help was appreciated and he was made much of. My mother never minded.

But on this occasion my mother did complain that it was a bit much of Frau Gietzen to expect my father to come running whenever he was required, and particularly unreasonable to ask him to interrupt his holiday and spoil the family enjoyment.

However, assuring her that it really was necessary and that he would be gone only a few days, he went. I have since realized that he had probably been summoned to hand over his trusteeship to an approved 'Aryan'. I don't know how long my father left us alone at Sieben Urlei, but it seemed a long time to me, and I am sure my mother felt lonely and slighted.

There were only a few other guests at the hotel. One of them was a Herr Holland, whom I remember as having very big teeth, a shiny forehead where his hair had receded, and tiny feet. He seemed a rather insignificant little man.

One evening when I was supposed to be in bed, I came downstairs into the lounge, wanting something or other, and there was Mummy with Herr Holland's arms around her shoulders. She was in the act of half-reluctantly trying to extricate herself. It really was nothing to make a fuss about: a middle-aged, solitary man comforting a young woman who was feeling a little sorry for herself. But to me the shock was absolute. I felt the whole, safe floor sliding away beneath me. I stood a second, open-mouthed, and then rushed from the room. I have since felt terribly sorry for my mother, but on this occasion I was horrid to her.

'I'll tell Daddy what you did!' I shouted. 'You're not my mother any more!' The Lord knows what other terrible things I said. I felt that she had betrayed my beloved father and I could think of little else until he returned. And I did tell him then, giving vivid details of Mummy's misdemeanour. I don't quite know what I expected. I was waiting for some sort of dramatic reaction, but all he did was laugh, a little uncomfortably, I thought, as though it was of no account. I think I felt relieved and disappointed at one and the same time. He tried hard to reassure me that all was well, for I imagined the worst, whatever that might be. Deep down, however, I still felt uneasy and restless and hovered about outside their room, and soon after heard them having a quiet heart to heart talk. 'So perhaps it wasn't all that unimportant,' I thought, and felt miserable. Lotte, who was still little, felt and saw none of this, and so I had no one with whom to share my troubled thoughts.

That holiday I stumbled on more disturbing discoveries. The kitchens were a little way apart from the main building. One morning I went there to get a drink. The door stood ajar and I heard Mummy's voice saying, '. . . of course, but my husband was married before . . .'

I did not stop to hear any more, but quietly withdrew. All I felt was incredulity and incomprehension. I told myself I must have misheard, yet knew I had not. An abyss of insecurity opened beneath me. I went for a long walk and hid away for the rest of the day and was silent and moody. My mother, who had been speaking to our hostess, did not know that I had overheard, and I was quite unable to speak about it to anyone.

I looked at my parents in a new light and started observing them. Doubts and suspicions troubled me. Was I Mummy's child, or was she my stepmother? And the word stepmother held all the gruesome associations of Grimm's fairy tales. Was Lotte her true child and were the two of them in league against me?

Then I would feel rage against my father. How *could* he love my mother if he had already loved someone else? Conflicting emotions and terrors tumbled through me. Whose child was I? Had they lied about my age? I suddenly started irritating inquisitions about my birth and the date of my birth and wanting to see my birth certificate. My parents must have wondered what on earth was the matter with me. I was sullen and secretive and unhappy for much of the remainder of the holiday, though, of course, there were moments when I forgot my troubles, such as one afternoon when we chanced upon a thicket of raspberries, as big as cherries, downy and sweet, and we gorged ourselves all afternoon, my father looping down the inaccessible branches with his stick.

But after that holiday nothing was ever *quite* the same again. It had rocked the absolute stability of my childhood. For a long time I could not speak about it, although I was longing to. I simply did not know how to put the turmoil inside me into words. In the end I just blurted out accusingly at my father, 'You have been married before!'

Again that uncomfortable laugh. But explanations followed, protestations of love, assurances that I was their child, Mummy's and his, that he loved Mummy very much, just as much as he had loved Klara, Klara, the woman in the white dress in the portrait. But though I lapped up these assurances, I wanted it not to have happened. And I could not quite recapture that old comforting sense of impregnable security. The safe landmarks had shifted, the world seemed alien and unpredictable.

I took a new interest in the portrait of Klara and started more inquisitions. I hated her for having possessed Daddy before us, knowing that it hurt him when I said I hated her. I could not feel that love was divisible. I kept pestering anyone who might know stories relating to Klara, hoping against hope that he had not really loved her. But all the stories dwelt on his devotion to her.

I now know that I had no need to doubt my parents' affection for each other, and when, some time ago, there came into my possession some poems that my father had written to Klara, I found them very moving and was ashamed of my early resentment of her.

6 Tensions

Everyone and everything seemed to be changing subtly. The enfolding timelessness of childhood wavered and faltered and its continuity was broken by intangible fears and uncertainties. No doubt I should have experienced something of the sort at about that time, simply because I was growing up, but instead of the sense of emergence and wider possibilities, I felt as though things were closing in on me. But this feeling was so confused and vague that I could not have expressed it.

Before I myself became aware of tension in the streets, I sensed that things were worrying my parents. I remember a great deal of talk about the *Wahltag* (election day). That must have been as far back as 1932. The name of Hitler was already very familiar and I knew that my parents dreaded his coming to power. I was surprised to find that some of the children with whom I played in the street, obviously echoing their parents, expressed the opposite view. I recall great gloom in our house when the election results were announced, though I am sure that my father did not recognize their full significance. Perhaps it was rather that he refused to do so; he loved Germany, its dark pine forests and mountains, and was steeped in its literature and history. I think he could not bring himself to believe the evidence of what was happening all around him. Meanwhile friends and relatives read the signs more clearly and some left for America,

England, Holland or Belgium at about this time.

After Hitler came to power things became worse. The pace changed imperceptibly at first, then faster and faster. There were no Jews living in Gerresheim, as far as I knew, (except the Heimbachs, a quiet, middle-aged couple) and as my father was respected in the district and the neighbours were, on the whole, decent people, the anti-Semitic campaigns were slow to affect us seriously.

But propaganda was already blatant. The papers all carried cartoons lampooning the Jews with enormous, grotesque noses, furtive or greedy faces and big, slobbering lips.

Very gradually people started withdrawing from contact with us. My father had the pride to accept this and not put them into any difficult or compromising situations. But I had to learn this sense of pride and dignity of not going where I was not welcome. I simply could not understand what was going on and resented the ostracism.

There was a very pleasant family living in our street with two children, Helmut and Eva. Lotte and I had always been invited to Eva's splendid birthday parties and I looked forward to them each year. Then one year the party took place without us.

People still greeted my parents, some openly, others surreptitiously. Then gradually those who had greeted us surreptitiously stopped altogether and avoided us, and those who had greeted us openly became more guarded. Then they too stopped altogether.

Aryan children were exhorted to join the BDM (League of German Girls) and the Hitler Youth. My best friend, Ella, started to become friendly with a newcomer to the district, Giesela, who was older than us and an enthusiastic member of the BDM. She felt it her duty to see that I was treated as a Jew ought to be.

At first I only sensed that I was less welcome in the street games; then some of the other children became actively hostile, teasing and baiting me and pushing me about when I was on roller-skates, so that I no longer liked going out to play. For a while Ella stood by me, despite Giesela's disapproval. Ella's mother was a forceful woman, who thought all this Hitler business nonsense and condemned it heartily at first. But gradually pressure from our contemporaries became too strong for Ella; she started coming to play with me only when she knew Giesela was away. But it wasn't the same any more; the free and easy intimacy had gone. Finally she stopped coming round altogether.

One afternoon, after I had noticed the children clustering and whispering, looking at our house, Ella walked up the steps, rang the bell and asked if I would come out to play. And I was afraid. I told Mummy to say that I was out. I watched Ella leave and, sure enough, Giesela and her crowd materialized from where they had been hiding round the corner. It left me rather afraid of them all.

I also remember an occasion when I had been out on my roller-skates and wanted to go back indoors. A bunch of boys and girls, some of whom had been my playmates and others who were complete strangers, sat on our doorsteps barring my way. They didn't say anything at all, but sat there looking at me mockingly, waiting. I felt completely helpless, but did not want them to see me cry or shout for Mummy. It was only when the occupant from the flat upstairs came home and wanted to get past, that I managed to slip in with him. I was very upset and frightened.

This sort of thing went on more and more. Parents who were not active Nazis and disapproved secretly, no doubt told their children not to take part, but not to interfere either. 'Just keep out of it.' It was not wise to show sympathy to Jews. Some people came and told my parents privately how terrible they felt about it all, but explained that in public they had to be 'discreet'.

At school the class no longer stood up and chorused, 'Good morning, Fräulein Rätchen!' when the teacher came in; instead we had to stand up, thrust out our arms and shout, 'Heil Hitler!' I never quite knew whether to join in or not. I knew Hitler was evil and the cause of all our troubles, but felt afraid not to raise my hand. Fräulein Rätchen, with her customary perspicacity, told me quietly one day that I need not do it. Instead of the little hymn or folksong with which we used to start the day, we now had to sing 'Deutschland Deutschland über Alles', 'Horst Wessel' or other patriotic or Nazi songs.

Already by 1935 Jewish children were forbidden to attend secondary schools. In 1936 they were also turned out of the *Volksschulen*, the state primary schools. This was particularly serious as there was no tradition of sectarian education in Germany and no alternatives existed. I had to go to a school especially set up by the Jewish community of Düsseldorf, and that was over an hour away by tram with two changes. My sister, then six years old, who had only just started at the *Volksschule* in Gerresheim, was too delicate for these daily journeys. Fräulein Rätchen, that sensible and courageous woman, who had been my teacher for four years, managed to take Lotte into her class, with the headmaster turning a blind eye. Lotte was a very bright little creature, lively and intelligent, and everyone was fond of her. There were no other Jewish children in Gerresheim, so that her attendance at the school went unobserved for a time and Fräulein Rätchen kept a close watch on any signs of persecution.

But in 1937 the risk became too great for the teachers. Complaints had been received from parents who were party supporters and Lotte had to leave and travel with me to the school in the Kasernenstrasse, next door to the synagogue. This school, created to meet the immediate need, was staffed with good teachers – they had, like the children, been thrown out of the state schools – and was very purposeful. The syllabus was designed as a preparation for emigration. Languages were given priority and Hebrew was compulsory. All the time children were leaving to emigrate with their families. Sometimes even the teachers, devoted and dedicated as they were, went. Every morning we would look round the class and notice new gaps. By 1938 the numbers were dwindling rapidly, and with it our restlessness increased.

None of the other children lived as far out as I did, but I had been given a new leather attaché case with a brass clasp and lock and that made me feel very important; so did the tram-pass in its stiff cellophane cover with my photograph. Once I got used to them, I quite enjoyed the journeys in the jolting trams, except in winter when it got dark early and often was very cold. But thinking back on it now, it must have been very worrying for my parents to have a ten-year-old girl travelling from Gerresheim to the Kasernenstrasse with two tram changes that involved crossing busy road-junctions and the possibility of facing racial 'incidents'.

I found the school a big change from Gerresheim. For one thing the children seemed different. They were Jewish children. They were bright-eyed and volatile; discipline was not strict and regimented. Some children were pushy and cheeky and the competitive spirit was strong. The atmosphere was far less formal than in German state schools and the convention of modest self-effacement was forgotten. Children called out their answers eagerly and knew how to assert themselves. They were intelligent and ambitious and since the older ones realized that this was their last chance of preparing for a very hostile world, they were eager to absorb as much as they could. Instead of the larking and time-wasting that one finds in most schools, there was a great sense of urgency. One of the first to leave was a handsome, dark-haired boy, tall and mature for his age. He had no doubts about where he was going – to Israel. He was one of the early young Zionists who, together with his elder brother, went to one of the first kibbutzim and on his arrival he sent our class a postcard.

Among the children at the school were the sons and daughters of families that still had plenty of money and those girls rang the changes of splendid wardrobes that I greatly coveted. But there was a complete cross-section of the Jewish population in the school, ranging from the Yiddish-speaking immigrants from Eastern Europe to the fully Germanized youngsters from old professional families. There had always been some snobbery and rivalry within the Jewish community; now the children of all sections – rich and poor, commercial and professional, liberal and orthodox – were thrown together and obliged to get on. But of course, the isolation from their fellow-citizens was increased, and with it the likelihood of persecution.

I don't remember my years at this school so well. I never really felt that I belonged. There was an air of unease and imperman-ence. I couldn't settle down to the new studies and I don't think I did very well. Although there were lessons in English and maths on the syllabus, when I later came to these subjects in England, they seemed new to me, as though everything I had learnt during those two years had been obliterated from my mind. Perhaps I had wiped them out along with other memories.

I do, however, remember some of the children quite clearly. The name of Norbert Zuckermayer sticks in my mind, because I fell for him headlong. I thought he looked wonderful: blue eyes, long lashes, light brown curls and a ravishing smile. I tried everything in my power to attract his attention, but I was very immature, gawky and still quite flat-chested, and certainly Norbert took little notice of me. He had eyes only for a girl called Lilo, who had charm and poise and whose figure had bumps and curves and who always wore the most fascinating clothes. I envied her and wondered what it was that attracted all the boys to her side; she was very quiet and unruffled.

I had made one very good friend there, Inge Lewin, the daughter of a lawyer. Once when the school had a half-holiday, Inge and I arranged that we would both bring our new ice-skates with us and go to the outdoor ice-rink after morning school. But when we got to the entrance of the rink we were confronted by a large notice: DOGS AND JEWS NOT PERMITTED. We hesitated. We were by then used to seeing 'No Jews here!' notices everywhere. We had been looking forward to skating, it was a sunny afternoon, a school holiday and such opportunities were rare. The temptation was overwhelming. There were so many people going in; it was not likely that anyone would know us, and besides, we considered that neither of us looked particularly Jewish; we both had blue eyes and light brown hair. So, after deliberating, we decided to go in. At first I felt a little nervous in case we should be recognized and denounced; then we grew more confident and had a thoroughly enjoyable afternoon.

When I told Daddy about our expedition, mentioning the notice, he became very grave. I suspect he realized how dangerous it had been for us to ignore the notice, but did not wish to alarm me, for he did not mention that aspect of it at all. Instead he tried to instil in me a sense of pride and dignity, and the importance of not going where I was unwelcome. I thought it all so unfair – not to be able to go skating.

Sunday, which had been my favourite day with its excursions to the *Gerresheimer Schweiz*, became for me a day of dread, a day to keep indoors and away from the windows. It had become a habit for the Brownshirts to start marching through the streets on Sunday mornings. The SA and sometimes the SS marched in automated rows, flinging their arms and jackbooted legs into the air, with their leather belts and swastika armbands and leather straps under their mouths, shrieking their Nazi songs with blood-curdling fervour.

At first they kept to the main streets, but later they penetrated even to quiet residential streets like ours, and their jackboots beat a rhythmical, slapping tramp on the metalled road. People, particularly children, used to run out to watch the parade and to shout, 'Heil Hitler! Heil Hitler!' saluting with stabbing arms.

Others deliberately stayed indoors, not really approving of this noisy display. If a Jew should have the misfortune to be on the street during a march his life was not safe. If he was wise he would hide in a doorway until the marchers had gone. If anyone in the crowd did not salute, Nazi supporters would set on him, but Jews would be attacked if they *did*, so they were not safe either way.

My mother's father, a bluff, well-built man of nearly seventy, had been set on by young Nazi thugs in the post office of his home town of Pirmasens, and left concussed and bleeding. I always feared for my father, who insisted on speaking out. I still marvel that he went unmolested at that time. Whether he was frightened or not, I don't know, but he continued to travel to town each day and often visited Jewish friends. Some of them were preparing to emigrate and needed help to organize their affairs, particularly if the head of the family had been arrested or had already gone abroad to prepare the way for his dependants. As time went on this took up more and more of my father's time and I used to hear my mother complain, 'Why don't you see to your own family?'

But he was reluctant at that stage to face the prospect of having to start again at the age of sixty-four, and of being, at least for a start, dependent on the charity of others. I could never go to sleep in those days until I heard my father come home. I would lie in the dark while Lotte was already breathing peacefully, waiting, hearing my heart thumping, and not knowing what I feared. I used to strain my ears for the footsteps in the outer hall, the moment's pause on the threshold and the sound of the key being inserted in the lock; then the weight of fear dropped off me. I would be out of bed like a rocket, my arms flung round Daddy. Often he looked so sad and strained. He tried to hide it from me, but his dejection communicated itself; it seemed palpable. His eyes had a veiled look and there was that treble crease between his brows, which I watched like a barometer for signs of his mood, watched it grow deeper and deeper. After a little chat and a little supper with him I would go back to bed reassured and fall asleep at once.

I had the same anxieties for Mummy. I behaved rather like a sheepdog rounding up the family, never content until we were all safely together indoors. I remember vividly those winter evenings when I got back from school in town. It got dark early. Whereas previously I had raided the pantry if Mummy was out when I got home, and unconcernedly settled down to reading, playing, or doing my homework, I now hurried in, 'Mummy! Mummy, are you in? Mummy? Lotte?' If there was no answer I would throw down my satchel and rush out of the house like a whirlwind. I chased down our street, across the road, down the next street and into the Benderstrasse, the main shopping street, peering into the shops as I ran, looking for her familiar face.

Panic made me pant and sometimes weep. '*Where* is she? Where *is* she?' I would mumble frantically to myself as I ran from lamplit shop to lamplit shop. Not at Portens's the baker's. Nor at the butcher's . . . the greengrocer's, the grocer's. Not at *this* one, perhaps at the other one round the corner? No, not there!

'Where can she be? Oh please God, let me find her, make her appear *now*!' I would feel sick with panic and running. Sometimes it would be drizzling and even today wet lamplight staining the pavement can bring a shadow of this anxiety. I had loved the lamplit streets, the friendly shops looking out into the murky winter evenings. It was odd how the very things I had loved now turned against me, and in some strange way increased my fears.

When finally her familiar shape materialized, her brown velour coat with the fur collar, her shopping basket on her arm and Lotte trotting beside her, then the panic evaporated and I felt drained. But I could never express what I felt. I was, in fact, ashamed of my childish behaviour and so I would merely say accusingly. 'I couldn't find you *anywhere*. Where were you? I looked everywhere.'

But that did not convey the relief I felt at seeing them, or the torture I had been through only a minute earlier.

'But you know I often go shopping at this time,' she would answer. 'I went to the delicatessen to get some of those herrings you and Daddy like so much and then I had to go to the haberdasher's to get some buttons.'

I had not thought to look there. I would next time.

At about this time everyone was supposed to have *Eintopfgericht* on Sundays. It was part of the 'guns before butter' programme and meant that everything you ate for the main meal had to be cooked in one pot to save fuel. The Brownshirts and other party members used to make spot checks to see whether the policy was being obeyed; there would be exhortations and chivvyings and sometimes arrests. Arrested Jews did not always return.

Eintopfgericht duly replaced chicken and rice, but the Brownshirts did not call on us. Later still there were checks on whether people were listening to foreign broadcasts on the wireless, but we did not have one.

Of course, we had long ceased to have any living-in maids, and the last of a succession of 'helps' in the house was Frau Ortman. I remember her well. She looked white, as though powdered with flour, with pale blue eyes and silky ivory-coloured hair. She had trouble with her feet and walked in a peculiar way, as though neither her toes nor her ankles had any joints. She was a very good, highly principled person and came to us in spite of her husband's disapproval. She had one daughter, Irmgard, with thick fair plaits, who came with her mother during the holidays to play with us. Frau Ortman was a tower of strength to my mother, both in practical matters and morally, because of her loyalty. When at last she ceased to come, it was because of my father's refusal to have her any more, as she might be endangering herself. Even then she continued to come irregularly to help us out. We could not stop her. Later, when Irmgard had to join the BDM, Frau Ortman was very upset, as she hated the Nazis.

Of course, I did not know the full significance of all these changes, but there was no need to tell me in so many words. From the whispered conversations, from the general attitude of people and friends I sensed that something mysterious and frightening was threatening us.

At the same time I was going through a self-assertive phase and was often argumentative and cheeky to my mother. I recall one incident when I was guilty of distressing my mother unnecessarily. The inevitable confrontations between parent and growing child were exacerbated by the strained atmosphere. My mother had a great deal to cope with and asked me to clean the entrance hall. As house-owners it was our responsibility to see that the spacious hall of black and white marble tiles and steps was kept clean. She gave me a bucket full of soapy water, a scrubbing brush and a cloth and asked me very nicely to get on with it. (I must have been insufferably spoiled and writhe as I recall the episode.) I felt the task to be beneath my dignity. Me kneel down and scrub the floor like any char? Suppose someone came and saw me? I refused . . . There was a scene. I became more truculent still. Then my mother lost her temper and throwing the wet cloth at my feet, she marched back into the flat, slamming the door shut behind her. I was left locked out with the bucket beside me. For a while I sulked away. But Mummy's loss of temper had frightened me. It was so unlike her usual calm and unruffled behaviour. Finally I knelt down resentfully and rather inadequately washed the floor, snivelling to myself as I did so. Of course, my mother was very upset and my father gave me a serious talking to. Had times been different, he said, he would most certainly have sent me into 'service' to strangers for a year, before allowing me to study.

'Before you can hope to give orders you must learn to obey; you must learn humility,' he admonished.

There remained a constraint between my mother and me for some days. I often thought of this incident after we were separated.

All these anxieties and tensions were bad enough, but there was far more serious trouble with my father's work. It became impossible for him to write as a theatre critic: a Jew could not presume to discuss or criticize the arts of the Third Reich.

Soon there was a campaign to have Jews sacked from 'Aryan' firms. The publishers, Lintz, could not ignore the pressure entirely and it was arranged that my father should no longer put in a personal appearance at the office, but do most of his work at home. This limited what he could do and his salary was reduced in consequence. The activities of my father and his co-managing director were closely watched and reported, for there was now a spy in the very heart of the camp.

His own secretary, Fräulein Heidrich, had been persuaded to become a Nazi supporter and could be relied on to report on what went on in the office. Fräulein Heidrich's defection was a sad blow to my father: she had given him many years of loyal service and he had greatly valued her work. She had played with us children and allowed us to tinker on her typewriter on our infrequent visits to Daddy's office when we were smaller. We were all of us very shocked.

Gradually, as Nazi pressure became more insistent, the amount of work allocated to my father diminished still further and there were several more downward revisions in salary. Then, with changes in the personnel of the board, my father's fellow managing director was unable to resist the pressure and it was suggested it would be better for everyone if my father considered retiring early.

A hint was enough. My father retired from the firm that had been half his life. His pension was less than it would have been, but it was still comfortable – until new laws restricted pensions to Jews and eventually forbade them altogether.

A friend subsequently told me that in fact it would have put the firm in great difficulty to have got rid of my father at once, since he was, in effect, totally responsible for the editorial side and consequently indispensable until someone could be initiated into the work.

Of course, my parents tried to conceal from us the full extent of their worries, but while these changes were going on, I used to see my father coming home earlier and earlier from the office, his shoulders stooping, his eyes bleak and preoccupied, and his walking stick, which used to dance a joyful descant on his steps, now following them tamely.

Apart from the loss of income, there were new expenses. The *Judensteuer*, a levy falling exclusively on Jews, was instigated. Capital was not safe either: Jews had to surrender all gold and silver to the German authorities. The night before taking away our family silver and the large inscribed tray his firm had given him on his fiftieth birthday, my father brought out the old leather casket of family heirlooms. We gazed sadly at the glittering collection. I don't think there was anything of exceptional value, but there were many beautiful antique objects and stones in fine old settings, and most of them had family stories attached to them. Here was the golden love-knot, a brooch his mother had worn on the Sabbath. There was a twisted golden snake-ring with emerald eyes, which had belonged to Klara. Saddest of all, my father had to part with his dented gold watch and chain, which had become so much part of him. He had never worn a wrist-watch.

Lotte and I were indignant at having to hand over our god-fathers' gifts. Mine had presented me with a solid gold spoon on every birthday – there were twelve already – and Lotte had a little sack of gold coins from hers. We felt tempted to retain this or that, but it was not worth the risk.

To help make ends meet our flat was divided up and half of it let off. Willy Karp, a young film director, moved in with his wife. But it was necessary to sell securities too, and I remember my father sitting for hours over endless columns of calculations in his tiny, neat figures. He comforted himself with the knowledge that his life insurance, in which he had invested a great deal, since his wife was so much younger than himself, remained as a final security for his family. In the end even that had to be capitalized and consumed.

It was in those days that one discovered one's true friends. In Gerresheim there were really in the end only the Röttger family, the Karps and Dr Paulson.

Karl Röttger was a remarkable man: schoolteacher, poet and writer of great perception and sensitivity. He was a member of the Charon Circle of poets and is recognized today as one of the foremost of German writers of the twenties and thirties, but many of his books were suppressed during the Third Reich. He suffered very much at that time for his decency and loyalty. Already life at school became difficult, because of his complete rejection of Hitlerian ideas. Spies reported that foreigners (English college students on exchange visits with his daughters) frequented his house and that he consorted with Jews. His phone was tapped and when my father rang him he always took the precaution of announcing himself by the name of Rhode, one of his early pseudonyms. Karl Röttger was frequently harangued by a Brownshirt *Ortsgruppenleiter* (district group leader) by the name of Wesch. Though barely literate he told Röttger what and how to write, suggesting he visited the pub to make contact with 'decent Germans'. Instead Karl Röttger insisted on greeting my father and mother at the tram-stop, even raising his hat, so that my father finished up by going out of his way to avoid him in public, knowing how he endangered himself.

The Röttgers had two daughters and a son. The son, Helmut, although a studious boy, was not allowed to go to university, since he had not been a member of the Hitler Youth. He was obliged to go into an *Arbeitslager* (work camp) and eventually to join the army. The two girls, Gerda and Rotraud, then about eighteen and twenty, had refused to join the BDM or any other Nazi organization. Rotraud was studying medicine and Gerda chemistry. Both refused to conform despite disadvantages and later even danger. The mother, Hella Röttger, was the same and came to see us at night. That family's friendship and moral support were a source of strength to my parents in those terrible times.

Gustav Lindemann also proved a loyal friend. He and his wife, the actress Louise Dumont, had founded the *Düsseldorfer*

Schauspielhaus (theatre) and made it a famous centre for avant-garde drama in the twenties and the home of the state theatre. He helped by offering my father the job as archivist after he had resigned from his firm.

Lindemann's family had Jewish connections and he had therefore retired from public life to a retreat in Bavaria. The archives consisted of papers to do with the theatre, his own life and that of Louise Dumont, who had died in 1932. He wished the archive to be created in her honour. The mass of material was in appalling chaos, but the work was a godsend. The pay was not much, but it helped and, equally important, my father was kept busy. He had known both the Lindemanns very well and been involved with the progress of their theatre. As with everything he undertook, my father became absorbed in the task, and the archives (eventually finished by other hands) have since been presented to the city of Düsseldorf.

Each day now seemed to bring new miseries. My lovely cousin Margot, so gentle and kind, had died at only twenty-nine. She had suffered from a heart complaint since her teens. For several years she had been deeply in love with a young doctor, Hugo Lichtenstein, who repeatedly asked her to marry him. For a long time she refused, because she felt she would be an invalid and might be a burden to him. Finally she gave way to his insistence that they should take their chance of happiness. After the wedding they lived together for three intensely happy weeks and planned to emigrate to England.

Suddenly, for no accountable reason, Hugo was arrested by the Gestapo. This blow was more than my cousin's heart could stand. She fell ill and although after a few weeks Hugo was released, Margot never recovered and died a few days later. He was shattered by her death and felt in some way responsible for it. (Later Hugo did go to England, where he was interned on the Isle of Wight for several years.)

One morning we received very disturbing news concering my Uncle Walter, my mother's younger brother. I did not know him very well, but I remember him vaguely when, as a little girl, I was very frightened by the sight of his wall-eye, which glared balefully at me. He had lost the sight of it as a small boy when he was hit by a stone from a catapult.

Walter, as the only boy and the youngest of his family, had been rather spoiled and my mother often ruefully said that he got away with everything. The two girls were not trained for any profession, but Walter went to university to study law. There he added a large, dashing *Schmiss* (sabre-scar) to his wall-eye. In spite of – or perhaps because of – these disfigurements he seemed attractive to women and was very susceptible himself.

He practised law successfully in Munich, but made no secret of his opposition to Nazism, even campaigning openly through the press and when that became impossible, through pamphlets. And so they were out to get him. A pretty 'Aryan' girl was used as a decoy and had no difficulty in persuading Walter to kiss her in a public park. That constituted *Rassenschande* (race-desecration). The Secret Police did not arrest Walter on the spot, but waited for him outside his flat. On his way home he was warned, and abandoning all his possessions and stopping only to borrow some money from a friend, he took the train to Czechoslovakia. Now he wrote to tell us of his trouble and flight. Though upset by the news, my parents were glad that he had escaped with his life and liberty. After a time in Czechoslovakia, Walter started practising law again, and wrote articles and pamphlets attacking the Nazis and their regime. He was still doing so in 1938 when Czechoslovakia was invaded by the Germans.

Those days filled me with fears of vaguely understood dangers, fear not just for myself, but for my parents, for Lotte. I never was quite at ease. Certain moments of intense panic seem, in retro-spect, to have dominated my days, although there must have been many occasions of carefree and happy distraction. But my parents' anxiety could not be hidden from us children, however hard they tried. And if they felt helpless, floundering and afraid for the future, the very foundations were rocking for me. Why this was, why to be Jewish brought this misery and fear to us, I could not understand.

At home I used to be frightened and restless as soon as dark came, unless our Venetian blinds were rolled down tightly without any cracks between the slats. I wanted to shut out the grey, fearsome streets with jackbooted Brownshirts who stamped about like robots, marching, shouting, saluting, red-faced, with wild and bloodshot eyes. At least, that is how they appeared to me. Danger was outside. At home we were safe – I thought.

7 The Ninth of November

It must have been three or four o'clock in the morning, when
suddenly I was ripped out of my sleep by the sound of smashing
crockery and glass. On and on it went. At first I thought I must be
dreaming still; it was an impossible sound in the dark and sleeping house. It seemed as though I lay there listening for several
minutes of incredulity, but it can only have been seconds. Now it
sounded as though the whole china cupboard had been hurled
down, with everything in it exploding. It was coming from the
kitchen. I don't know what I thought: burglars, an earthquake?

'Lotte!'

She too was awake and both of us were out of our beds, out of
our room, flying into our parents' room a few doors along the
passage. But it was no longer a haven. My father in his nightshirt
stood speechless beside the bed – he was on his way to fetch us –
my mother was sitting up, her black hair streaming over her
shoulders, her eyes wild with fear. She gathered us into the bed
with calming sounds. Seconds later there burst into this room a
horde of violent monsters, their faces contorted into raving
masks of hatred, some red, some pale, all screaming and shouting, eyes rolling, teeth bared, wild hands flailing, jackboots
kicking. They were wielding axes, sledgehammers, stones and
knives. They rushed about the room smashing, throwing,
trampling. It seemed to me that there were hundreds of them

bursting through the door, though I believe there were, in fact, only a dozen.

A chair hurtled into the wardrobe mirror, glass flying everywhere. Crouching in bed I saw a monster with a knife-blade shining, screaming towards a painting on Daddy's side of the bed. It was a valuable painting, a very beautiful landscape in which my father took great joy. Around me there was tumult, noise, confusion, but suddenly all my attention became fixed. My whole being became focused upon my father's pathetic figure in his nightshirt, moving towards the painting as if to shield it, 'Das nicht, das nicht!' I heard him plead. And then, just as in a nightmare in which everything is happening in slow-motion and in which one is paralysed and helpless at the crucial moment, I saw one Nazi pick up a large marble slab from the smashed dressing-table top. He raised it high above his head. In that split second, as he threw it across the room with all his might at my gesticulating father, I had a momentary vision of him being smashed to the ground, but my father had ducked instinctively and retreated to the bedside, watching, now speechless, as another Nazi dug his knife-blade deep into the canvas, slashing and hacking as though he wanted to fell the staunchly-painted summer oak.

Now fear became a living thing, fear for the life and safety of my parents, who represented my own safety. It was like drowning. I sat numbed and in shock, watching without a sound as axes flew into the screaming wood of chests and wardrobes. The one who had hurled the marble slab hardly stayed to watch the result, but frothing at the mouth he found new sport in splintering doors and window-frames and driving his axe into the wall and floorboards.

By now the Brownshirts themselves were wading in glass and torn wood. This room seemed to me the nucleus of their raging madness, although by now only three or four creatures remained, the others were busy elsewhere, destroying. Sometimes I was aware of sounds from other parts of the house, sometimes all my senses were concentrated on the wild spectacle before me. With nothing left to smash in this room except the bed, a large, sweating pig of a Brownshirt advanced towards our bed and once again I seemed to be experiencing what had not yet happened, but was about to happen, and I was unable to move or utter a sound. My mother's legs were stretched beneath the sheet (the eiderdown had long ago been ripped away). I saw the monster raise his axe about to sink it into the middle of the bed and – right through my mother's legs! Did I scream, or only think I did? Again, as when my father ducked under the slab, by reflex my mother pulled up her legs just as the blade sank through the sheet into the mattress. I think I was utterly numb. Yet all the while the sights and sounds about me etched themselves into my mind. They are as vivid today as they were then.

Then there came to the side of our bed a small man, outwardly the same: brown shirt, leather belt and jackboots, but he had a face, not a distorted mask and he had human eyes that saw our fear. He bent low and whispered, 'Children don't look, don't look children. Hide your eyes. I am sorry. I had to do it.'

And somehow he drew the fanatic horde of raving animals from our room, drew them away, smashing and slashing, into other rooms.

Quite suddenly our room was empty and we were all still alive. No one moved. The sounds continued awhile and then there was silence, though my mind still heard the noise. But there was silence, complete and sudden, with only the broken furniture groaning and settling into place. We listened to the silence for a long time, not daring to breathe, expecting them to return any minute to kill us all. But they did not return.

Of what followed immediately after this hurricane that had swept through our home and out again, I cannot remember anything clearly; either what we thought, or said, or did. All that remains is a series of pictures imprinted on my mind.

The most vivid, because to me the most shattering, is of my father slumped on a chair that had been overlooked in the kitchen beside the cooker, weeping quite shamelessly. My heart turned over and seemed to stop. Never in my whole life had I seen my father weep.

Other images succeed each other: the piano on its side, its guts ripped out and scattered on the floor like the bones and sinews of some huge animal; every single oil painting hanging in strips out of its frame or lying impaled on the spikes of upturned furniture; the huge painting of Klara slashed from corner to corner, her white dress in tatters; my mother's cherished collection of old china cups – all shapes and sizes, from many countries – not *one* left unbroken.

The delicate Meissen figures, Dresden bowls and Chinese vases lay in smithereens, the china fruits and flowers ground into the carpet by jackboots. Fine old leather-bound books were torn, the pages scattered; furnishings were slashed with the stuffing welling out like flesh; old oak and walnut tables and chairs were legless; the carpets hacked, curtains torn down, floorboards splintered and many windows smashed, with the cold black night crowding in.

Suddenly the silence was torn by a strident shrilling sound echoing through the house. The telephone. Ringing, ringing, ringing. Why doesn't it stop? Where *is* the telephone? We couldn't see it anywhere, yet it kept on ringing and ringing. We clambered about the living-room, but couldn't discover under which smashed pile of furniture it lay. At last we spotted a portion of flex firmly pinned underneath the huge piano. Impossible to get at. And still it continued ringing; a frightening sound from the hostile world outside. Or perhaps it was some friend trying to find out if we are all right? But how could anyone have known what had happened to us? At last it stopped, quite suddenly. That was frightening too. Who was it? What did they want?

Next Willi Karp, our tenant, who with his wife occupied the two rooms that had been separated off, appeared at our bedroom door and I heard him weeping noisily, embracing Daddy, saying, 'Oh I'm so ashamed. So ashamed . . . of my country . . . of myself.' He wanted reassurance and forgiveness for not coming out to help during the attack.

My father comforted him, 'You couldn't have done anything. Don't blame yourself. It's not your fault.'

'Oh I'm so ashamed to be German . . .'

It helped a little, to see his shock and feel his sympathy.

It had all been well organized. The Brownshirts had known exactly where to go and where not to go. They knew that the Karps' doors, on one side of our hall and apparently part of our flat, were not to be touched. They had been well briefed.

Later we learned how that came about. *Ortsgruppenleiter* Wesch, who tormented Karl Röttger because he was a 'high-brow' writer, had decided to distinguish himself by ensuring that Gerresheim was the first district in Düsseldorf to be *Judenfrei* (free of Jews). To that end he had imported a gang of Brownshirts from another district to 'pay us a visit and make a good job of it'. As a neighbour he was able to give them precise instructions.

I remember small comforts and kindnesses in the midst of the chaos: the Karps bringing us cups and warm drinks. There was not one whole cup left from which to drink, not a plate or saucer. But after that night we saw little of the couple. No one could blame them.

Finally there was nothing more to be done. We had wandered through the ruin of our home and there were still a few hours left before day. And miracle of miracles, the children's room had been left unscathed. Someone, as a token gesture, had toppled the wardrobe on which our doll's house stood, some of the toy peasant furniture was broken, but once we had raised up the wardrobe and cleared away the wreck of the doll's house, we found the rest of the room untouched. Lotte's and my bed were still whole. So Daddy and I lay down in my bed, foot to head, and Mummy lay down with Lotte in the other. There was a certain comfort in the inability to do anything, to think anything . . . Amid this chaos and at that time of night, battered and shaken, we had to lie down and rest, and I do believe that all of us slept a little from sheer emotional exhaustion.

The grey, tormented day came only too soon, when we had to get up, weary and frightened, and face our shattered home. We wandered through the ruins, through leaves of glass, curved like scimitars, trying to assess the damage, trying to find a single unsmashed cup, trying to extricate what we could, not knowing where to start and not knowing what was happening in the world outside. Was it only us? Was it safe to go out? What was happening? The phone kept ringing – people were still trying to get in touch. But still the murdered piano lay sprawled on top.

That day nobody went out. I think with Mr Karp's help the piano was lifted and the Röttgers were at last able to speak to us, but Daddy stopped them from coming to see us in daylight. In the evening Frau Röttger and her two daughters came, bringing food, crockery and warm clothes and, what is more, the feeling that we were not utterly alone in the world. They also brought us news of the terrible happenings everywhere during the past night. There had been a concerted attack on the Jews all over Germany on the night of the ninth of November 1938. All the synagogues and thousands of shops and homes had been wrecked. It became known as the *Kristallnacht*, or the 'night of (broken) glass'.

Later that evening, while moving around our parents' bedroom, all trying to restore a little order, there was a sudden surprised exclamation from Lotte. She was holding her leg, where a large, silvery-blue snail seemed to have embedded itself in her flesh just below the knee. She put her finger on it, trying to touch it, when suddenly the blood gushed out. A jagged shard of mirror had sprung at her while she was trying to lift something and had cut her leg, exposing sinews and bone. Once she saw the blood she starting howling. What were we to do at this time of night, not knowing whether Brownshirts were lurking outside? To call a doctor might compromise him. But clearly Lotte needed stitches; the wound gaped wide and the bleeding could not be stopped. Nobody wanted to be left alone in the house, so all four of us fled through the silent streets, Daddy carrying Lotte, Mummy supporting her legs, Lotte howling like a banshee, I keening by their side, till we reached the house of Dr Paulson. Would he see us, or turn us away?

Without question Dr Paulson ushered us into the house and unlocked the surgery. After stitching up Lotte's leg, he listened horror-struck to what had happened, and frankly expressed his revulsion and disgust with the Nazi movement. He was kind and tried to comfort and calm us. He told us when to return to have the stitches removed – it would, of course, have to be at night after surgery hours, but it was good to know that at least we would not be without medical attention if we needed it. In a way Lotte's accident was a salutary influence. It shook us out of our numbed state and galvanized us into positive action. All four of us were still together and well.

Many peole felt repungance at the Nazi lawlessness, but nobody dared say so in public. When my father called at the local police station to tell them what had occurred and to lodge an official complaint, the police were sympathetic and admitted that they disapproved of what had taken place, but they had received orders not to interfere. They were sorry, but they were powerless. So there was nowhere to turn. The Jews were outlaws.

It was November and quite cold and we had difficulty in

getting someone to come and mend our smashed windows. My father spent hundreds of Marks in getting carpenters to restore what could be salvaged from the wrecked furniture. I sensed the futility of it, but the fact that my parents felt it was worthwhile to re-establish our household in some sort of order, was reassuring. The gradual return of domestic routine helped us to cope with the shapeless days that followed. There was no school for us for the time being; the synagogue had been burnt down and the adjacent school sacked. Far from rejoicing in our enforced 'holiday', we longed for contact with our companions and the world outside.

One by one Jewish friends rang us. Most had suffered as we had, though some had been passed by. Others gave reports of friends injured or even murdered and of menfolk taken away, presumably to concentration camps. We considered ourselves lucky. And my father was soon busy helping those worse off than ourselves. Outwardly he still seemed unafraid. He went about by public transport as he had always done. He was constantly visiting friends in Düsseldorf, particularly the relatives of those who had been carried off, helping them with their preparations to emigrate. He never told my mother where he was going. 'It's best you don't know where I am,' he said. Once, when returning from a short walk, Mummy, Lotte and I noticed from the distance that a car was stationed outside our house. One was always afraid it might be the SS. We went away again and did not go back till some time later. The car had gone and did not return.

But my father had his little bag packed ready, in case they came for him. For me that little case embodied all my fears, uncertainties and uncomprehended threats. What was in it? 'Just bare necessities,' I was told. It was such a small case that it had no room for anything but 'bare necessities'. My imagination brooded darkly around the contours of that little case, that stood ready, packed, waiting – for what? It represented the culmination of all my fears.

At this time we were bombarded with telegrams from my Uncle Max in America and from my relatives in London, pleading with my father to emigrate, to send us out ahead.

'Yes, yes I will,' promised my father, 'but first . . .' But, of course, there were a thousand things to be attended to first.

Whenever he went into a public call-box – he dared not ring up people from home in case he should compromise them – I insisted on going with him. I hated the uncertainty of not knowing what was happening to him and couldn't bear to be left at home. I felt obscurely that the two of us were safe together. I would wait outside the telephone-box to see that no one would creep up and trap him inside.

When I saw his figure stooping now, coming down the street with his lagging stick and strained face, during those early days of 1939, I was moved with a deep love and pity for my father. But still there seemed a strength in him, an underlying love of life, a courage to face everything and with it the power of conveying hope. Perhaps it was this that made so many people come to him for comfort and advice and that made me want to keep close to him. But with all this helping others, he was too busy to help himself. Or did he not want to?

I think quite honestly my father was stunned. For the moment he floundered. It meant recognizing the utter hopelessness of life in Germany. Everything he had spent his life in building – a comfortable home, prospects for his family, a full and civilized way of life, full of friendships and the enjoyment of beautiful things and ideas – had been destroyed. How could he face such an absolute denial of his ideals? Perhaps the desertion by many who had been his friends was the worst thing. Perhaps, at sixty-four, he lacked a little of the resilience of younger men who were able to plunge impulsively into the uncertainties of a new life abroad. He could see only too clearly what it would mean to start afresh in another country at his age, without means of support, without language, and the thought that he might be dependent on the charity of others appalled him beyond anything. But could he not smell the strong stink of danger? My mother, my Uncle Max in America, my aunt and cousins in England, the Röttgers in Gerresheim, all urged him to swallow his pride, to stop repairing the damaged home, stop preparing and planning for an ordered exodus, but to leave while there was yet time. To go at once!

8 Preparations for Departure

My father could no longer resist these appeals. The family must prepare to leave. My mother started going to evening classes run by the Jewish community. These were an attempt to prepare women, most of them not used to earning a living, for a penniless fresh start. She went to courses in English and pastry baking. While this was going on my father set about trying to find means for an ordered departure, at the same time coping with the difficulties and uncertainties of each day and night.

All the time relatives were visiting us as a staging-post on their way abroad. My father was forever meeting trains, seeing trains off, and making last-minute promises to see to things that had been left undone. Uncle Hugo (the wine-merchant) brought his family from Stuttgart to stay with us before leaving for Baltimore. They too had been 'visited' on the *Kristallnacht* and Hugo, in desperation, had produced his First World War Iron Cross, as evidence that he was a loyal German. He got an extra beating for that.

Emigrating Jews were not allowed to take more than ten Marks out of Germany. We could not all fall on Uncle Max in Baltimore, who apart from having to support Hugo and his family until they established themselves, had already provided the necessary affidavit to enable them to enter the USA. 'We must not add to his burdens,' said my father.

It was tempting to smuggle out a few valuables, but apart from some of his best stamps, which he packed up in a little tin for a friend to carry, my father felt the risk was too great. Every day people left for Holland, England or America, and those who needed time to extricate themselves sent their children to relatives or friends abroad by one of the Children Transports that were being chartered by international Jewish organizations.

Then came the telephone call from America with the peremptory message, 'Send the children. There isn't much time left. Their affidavit is now in order.'

When my parents had taken the shattering decision to send us ahead, that too had to be done properly. Whirlwind preparations began. We must not find ourselves resented as a burden. We should not depend on others for clothes, bed-linen and so on. For a short while my mother was in her element, planning, buying, making our 'trousseau' for several years ahead. Where the money came from I can't think. But in the excitement of getting all these new clothes, I forgot the true purpose behind it and was swept up in the exhilaration of preparations.

A dressmaker came (a Jewish acquaintance) and we were fitted and measured and turned, while the old treddle sewing-machine went purring on. I remember that period vividly and with it almost every single garment that I was given. They were all my dearest dreams of dresses come true. In recent years money had not been plentiful and we had only been given one new wool dress each year at Christmas, but now suddenly we had three new wool dresses each, in exactly the style and material I loved. One consisted of a pleated skirt, buttoning onto a top with large mother-of-pearl buttons. The material was of fine wool in tiny wine and navy checks. Another (for best) was made of a colourful plaid material with a small white collar and a shiny, stiff, red bow in front, made of some marvellous unknown material, of which I was very proud. Another dress (to grow into) was cut in Mandarin style with beautiful hand-embroidery all round the upright collar and down the front. There were *Bleyle* dresses, winter coats, pleated skirts, numerous jumpers, some for immediate use, others for the following year, for we were growing fast. There were summer clothes, night-wear, shoes and boots, gloves and caps, underwear, socks and stockings and liberty bodices. That which wasn't new was carefully repaired and everything had to be name-taped.

Lotte and I, together with Mummy and Daddy, were busy

selecting those few toys and books which could be sent on. Many a tear was shed in the selection process. Two new cases were bought. Children going by Children's Transport were allowed only one substantial case each, and a single crate of used things could follow later; there was to be only one consignment. Gifts for my aunt and her family were also enclosed.

It began to feel like an adventure: all these wonderful clothes and these exciting preparations, and to travel across the sea to England. . . After all, we were going to my Tante Rosel and Onkel Ala. They were all right, and in any case, it was only going to be a short time before Mummy and Daddy would follow. They would come to England and then all together we would go to America. Really, it *was* exciting. I always imagined America in glossy technicolor like the vivid fruit-tin labels that Uncle Max printed and sometimes sent us.

'But you will come soon, won't you? *Very* soon?' I would plead.

And the answer would be reassuring, 'Yes, as soon as we can get our papers through and things arranged here.'

How I wished they would just pack their bags and come with us, *now*. There were other preparations too: in a casual sort of way Daddy would talk to us about what it might be like to leave home, the problems that might arise. He reminded us that he too had left home at thirteen, my age, to go into apprenticeship.

'You are old enough to know right from wrong,' he told us and adjured me not to be too selfish and to think of Tante Rosel and to help her in the house. Above all, he committed Lotte into my care; I was to be a mother to her, as she was still so young. He told us always to have faith in God and in Life and in their love for us. Hesitatingly he suggested that if anything troubled me that I didn't understand, I should consult Tante Rosel, or some other sensible woman, if she were not at hand.

At last everything was ready and we had received the notification that our Transport train was leaving Düsseldorf Station on 3 May 1939. I think it was the last but one Children's Transport that stopped to pick up in Düsseldorf. Those of my schoolfriends who had not already gone had literally 'missed the boat'.

The night before we left my father wrote a final poem into our autograph albums and my mother also wrote some loving lines. I was to read these again and again during the years that followed.

Before we left the house that morning, my father and my

mother laid their hands on our heads and blessed us, as they always did on Friday evenings, for the last time.

It was a very long train. I don't know how many children it was carrying, but it had come a long way, picking up children at different towns. I think that Düsseldorf was the last pick-up point. It all passed like a dream. I can't remember whether there were other parents seeing their children off – there must have been. I do remember when the unbelievable moment of separation actually came. We were all busy with the preoccupations of finding the right coach and compartment, of stowing the luggage. Then the last clinging embrace: my face against the familiar tweed of my father's coat and the comforting feel of my mother's fur collar.

Then we were on the train. We didn't cry then. We all knew we mustn't. Not Mummy either. She was so brave. I think Lotte and I waved goodbye happily, still hearing their last firm assurances: 'We're coming soon . . . in a few weeks. . .'

Then, as I saw their lonely figures receding as the train drew out, looking so forsaken after all they had done for us, I cried, but not for too long. There were so many new faces to take in, so much to think about, and then there was Lotte, weeping away beside me. 'Look after Lotte!' were their last instructions and I promised myself that I would. It was the least I could do, now we were on our own.

What I didn't know at the time, but learnt from Hella Röttger after the war, was that my father, anxious to see that we got safely across the border, had jumped on to the train at the very end, where it curved around a corner and we could not see from where we were, and had travelled on it all the way to the Dutch border. At the frontier, guards and some officers came into each carriage and questioned us about our luggage: were we carrying any valuable things? Some children had their cases opened, but all passed off quietly in our carriage. My father left the train as unobtrusively as he had got on, and watched it snake its way across the frontier into Holland and safety; a train full of children, full of hope, leaving behind the broken hearts of mothers and fathers, empty homes and a future of 'night and fog'.

9 Refugees

Of the journey I remember very little. There were children sitting beside us and opposite us; a blur of faces. But it was a strange journey: no larking or fooling about, as is usual on excusions where a lot of children are together. We were all subdued and thoughtful, wondering where we should end up and how it would all be.

We travelled by night-boat from the Hook of Holland to Harwich and from there by train to Liverpool Street Station where we were to be checked and claimed by our sponsors and relatives.

I faintly remember meeting my dear friend, Inge Lewin, (the girl with whom I had gone to the forbidden ice-rink) at Rotterdam. Her father had emigrated to Cuba and the rest of her family had left Düsseldorf just one month before us and were now waiting in Holland for permission to join him. My father had written, and now they came to see us as we passed through.

But the whole journey had a somnambulistic quality – train, boat, train, interspersed with endless standing in long, labelled files. I suppose that with all the excitement and emotional strain of farewells, frontier hold-ups and apprehensions, we were tired out.

The first clear picture that emerges is of our arrival very early in the morning at Liverpool Street Station, a vast glass dome swirling with steam, and of filing through a door into a great hall with windows high up in the walls and a grey light filtering through them. As we entered, our names were checked off a list and we were each given a packet of sandwiches, some chocolate and an orange. It's funny how children always remember food. Certainly this orange, round and brightly glowing in the grey surroundings, suddenly cheered me and brought back a sort of excitement and anticipation.

I suppose we were hungry by then, but I don't remember actually eating the orange. Perhaps I was still clutching it when we arrived at my aunt's flat.

It seemed hours and hours that we sat in that grey hall on wooden benches. I have an impression of a gallery where relatives and sponsors sat waiting for their charges. I think we must have been dealt with alphabetically, for we two Zürndorfers heard name after name being called and saw nearly all the children who had travelled with us leave.

But where were Tante Rosel and Inge? I could not see them in the gallery. What if they had not come? Would we be sent back, or would we have to stay in this depressing hall? Lotte began to fidget and weep. Then, when there were only a few unclaimed children scattered about the hall, our names were called: 'Hannele and Lotte Zürndorfer!'

We stood up and a lady led us to a desk where our labels were taken off our necks and we were handed over to our official English sponsor, Mrs Ettinghausen, a kind, smiling lady. And there stood Tante Rosel, small and anxious, and Inge. We were no longer baggages, numbers, labels, but children with a loving aunt who hugged and hugged us and took us away from that stuffy hall as soon as the formalities had been completed and the luggage collected. I looked back and the boy who had sat next to us on the bench was still there, looking so lost and lonely. I wondered what was going to happen to him.

We went by taxi and I kept thinking to myself, 'This is England!' We drove through crowded streets full of shops and people bustling about. All the notices were in English and all these people out there were talking English. It really was exciting! Then the taxi stopped in front of a large, cream-coloured villa fronted by a porch with flaking pillars. And out of the window at the very top of the house looked Uncle Ala, waving and pulling funny faces. When we had climbed the three flights of stone stairs, Ala tried hard to make us laugh, but he looked older and sadder than I remembered him and I felt a bit like crying. We were made so welcome and cousin Egon hopped excitedly from foot to foot and immediately started teaching us English, 'Good afternoon, girls,' he said. It was comforting to be with relatives. A telegram was dispatched to Mummy and Daddy.

Everything was so strange. It was a small attic flat and poor Inge, my cousin, was supporting not only her parents but also her brother Egon, who as an alien was unable at that stage to get a job. He was very gifted with languages and did all he could by giving lessons, while Uncle Ala earned a few shillings by doing some manual piece-work at home. In the past we had called him 'Uncle Joker', because he was always trying to make us laugh. He used to look at Lotte in a funny sort of way and within two seconds Lotte would be crying, smiling bravely and insisting through her tears, 'I'm not really crying.' It was meant to be funny, but it wasn't really and I know that Lotte was feeling a little apprehensive on that account. But this Uncle Ala was a much changed man. Indeed, we tried to cheer him up and egg him on into teasing us, he seemed so sad and depressed.

The little flat was in need of repair and cheerful paint, but we were told that the landlord wasn't much concerned about that. It was quite difficult for my relatives to fit us in. The living-room was a bit gloomy and overcrowded with furniture, and both the bathroom and lavatory were painted a sickly brown. None of the rooms was very spacious or well-lit and the flat seemed a long way from the street to us, who had been used to living at ground level. The back garden made a splash of green, but was reserved for the use of the ground-floor tenants.

Egon had given up his room to Lotte and me, and slept on the sofa in the living-room. Two beds had been borrowed for us and my father wrote to say that he was trying hard to get permission to send our beds and bedding. My parents felt so grateful and tried in every way possible to lighten the burden that our arrival must have constituted.

Naturally I did not appreciate fully how much extra work and hardship it meant for my aunt and her family, and often was not as helpful or contented as my parents' letters reminded me I ought to be.

My aunt, the youngest and only girl of the four Zürndorfer

siblings, adored my father, her favourite brother, and now she transferred her affection to us. She was a warm person, but in those days overworked, worried and not in good health. Neither she nor my uncle was young enough to take the drastic re-adjustments of emigration in their stride. She still had her silky black hair and prided herself on not being grey at all. She was lively and intelligent: 'the only person I know who is able to pronounce two words on top of each other', my father used to say, for she spoke very quickly, as though she could not com-municate her thoughts fast enough. When she tried to do the same in English the effect was very funny, with all her 'shs' and 'ths' getting jumbled up.

Uncle Ala, always rather quiet, bottled up his worries and brooded on his ineffectualness. He was a strange man and I never really understood him. He was highly intelligent, very modest and, I think, often misunderstood. Somehow he lacked drive and probably would have been happiest had he remained in South Africa working for a plantation. After he returned from there to Germany for the sake of his baby daughter, Inge, who suffered from the climate, he had had a go at all sorts of things without much satisfaction. But in spite of his brooding silences, I was very fond of him. He taught me the rudiments of chess during our days with him in Hampstead.

Inge had been a student in Germany in the early thirties. Politically aware, she had taken advantage of her British pass-port (from her birth in South Africa) and left Germany as soon as she had graduated in 1933. Now she was fully integrated and earning reasonably well as a social worker. Already in her late twenties, she had sacrificed a great deal. There was now not enough money for her to marry Kurt, a handsome young man who, like her, had a refugee family to support. They had known each other a long time, but for many years yet the marriage had to be postponed.

Although we slept in Egon's room it could not really be ours, because he had to use it in the daytime, and all his books and papers were there. There was very little room for our things and we had to be continually tidying them away. Of course, the whole arrangement was only a temporary stop-gap until my parents could collect us on their way to the USA, so we never settled down to think of the flat as home. But we were happy enough, because our relatives were kind and loving and did all they could in what must have been very difficult times.

In the mornings we would be woken very early by Egon, impatient to tell us his latest Jewish jokes about two characters called Mosche and Meusche. His bright eyes glinted hopefully, waiting for our laughter. Though we seldom understood the jokes we found his mimicry and endless clowning irresistible. With that encouragement there was no stopping Mosche's and Meusche's exploits. Then Egon, who had an exhaustive knowledge of opera, would illustrate his detailed accounts of Wagner's *Ring* with 'The Ride of the Valkyries', played on his ancient gramophone, until my aunt appeared in her nightdress, ordering him back to bed.

Egon adored his young cousins and certainly kept us amused. I often felt he would have made a good comedian. He also had an astounding gift for languages and had taught himself to speak fluent French, Spanish and Portuguese. His English was already very good and his vocabulary extensive, even though he had been in England only little more than two years.

Very soon after our arrival he started giving us formal English lessons to prepare us for school. All I knew when I arrived in England was 'good morning', 'thank you very much', 'strawberry jam' and 'porridge'; the sum total that remained of the English lessons at the Jewish school. My aunt, though she tried to speak English with us, found it difficult at fifty-seven and pretty soon lapsed into German or a droll mixture of the two languages, and my parents figured large in all her conversations.

Cards and letters from my parents started pouring in. During May and June alone there were more than thirty letters, all of them hungry for news, for the sight of our handwriting. Every postcard came with a pre-paid reply-section.

On 5 May, two days after our departure, when our separation seemed still unreal, my mother wrote:

> It is Friday evening and so quiet. Daddy, Opa and Oma [my maternal grandparents] are out and instead of frying my cut-lets, I shall quickly have a little chat with you. It's already one and a half days since you have been with our dear ones – think of all the things you will have to tell us! I am longing to hear your news. We have received your card from Rotterdam and the telegram and card from London and I am glad that every-thing is *prima* and *knorke*. [*Prima* and *knorke*, expressions of

enthusiasm, were the current slang of German school children. We had evidently used them in the card describing our journey, and here my mother seizes on them.] Did you manage to sleep all right on the boat?. . . If only I had a telescope and could quickly take a look at you . . .

Do you keep your things tidy? I would love to be able to tell you off, but everything is so tidy now, and nothing left lying about. But I hope it won't be necessary any longer for Tante Rosel or Ala to ask you to tidy up. Once you get into the habit of doing it yourselves, it will become quite easy and natural, and Tante Rosel won't have so much extra work.

The weather is lovely here. Have you unpacked your cases yet? You do remember what you are to wear for everyday and what for best? And always wear your aprons without having to be told. I wonder if I have said everything now?

On 6 May my father wrote:

I think my condition gives cause for concern. I want to be writing letters to you all the time, and receiving them too, of course. It's lucky you're not on the telephone. . . Mummy's letter, which I enclose, seems more like a questionnaire. . . I have one question, to be answered at once: did you arrive safely with all your cases and belongings intact? Once I know that, I can put in hand the sending of your beds. How are you sleeping at present?

My darling children, [wrote my mother] it is already eight days since the train carried you away. I was hoping to have a letter or card from you today, but I shall have to be patient till tomorrow, perhaps the postman . . .

And my father wrote a day later:

It was a great joy to us when your long letter arrived today. Mummy, of course, was already looking for it yesterday with the evening post. You should have seen the broad grin that spread across a proud mother's face (fathers merely smirk) at your description of our brats, dear Rosel. . .

In her letter my mother wrote:

What a pleasure when the postman brought your long letter from Hampstead. I can't last longer than three days without news. It is always the same here when one of your letters arrives: we all sit around the table while Daddy reads your letters aloud; only afterwards do I get them handed out to me, so that I can feast my eyes on your handwriting. Then it goes back into Daddy's wallet where he carries it around with him next to his heart, showing it proudly to friends who ask after you. . .

On 10 May my father wrote:

On Sunday afternoon at half-past four I said, 'It is now exactly 100 hours since we saw our children for the last time.' . . .and so you have been shown the sights of London town. Don't spoil the children, Rosel; it must cost you a great deal in bus-fares. . . .

Do you know what pleased me most in your letter, dear Hannele, the remark that you have not quarrelled with Lotte yet. Five whole days! As a reward I have sent off your copy of *Stern* . . . We enjoyed your vivid descriptions and drawings of your adventures in London. . .

My father also sent a letter containing an elaborate puzzle, with clues all based on long-standing family jokes, and conclusions that gave the birthplaces of 'the leading members of a famous family'. Prizes were promised for correct answers, and in the next letter they came: a sprig of camomile and a little poppy picked in the *Gerresheimer Schweiz*.

At that time their letters were still full of concern for small daily details. Thus my mother wrote:

. . .dear Rosel, please keep an eye on Hannele's bowels, she tends towards constipation. . . It is very cool here. I know, dear Rosel, you'll keep an eye on what they wear.

I always had to make sure that they dressed according to the weather. Hannele in particular, can be difficult about clothes. . . Please dear children, take care of your new coats; they have to last you a long time. If it's cool wear your Lodencoats. . .

And so Lotte and I were settling in with my relatives. It had been decided to give us a few weeks to acclimatize before sending us to school. We had already missed a great deal of schooling during the period after the pogroms, and so a week or two more did not matter. We went for short walks with Ala, who seemed to get very short of breath. I went shopping with Tante Rosel in Kilburn with huge, square shopping bags. I still remember to my shame, that on one occasion I conceded only very reluctantly and rather sulkily to lug one of those unsightly oil-cloth bags, bulging with cauliflowers, bread and potatoes.

We soon learnt our way around the streets of Swiss Cottage and I felt very proud when I was sent to the nearby parade of shops to buy butter, or milk at the Express Dairy, using my newly acquired English and struggling to come to grips with shillings and pence. Once I was sent to buy oranges and, pointing, I asked the assistant for 'six of those bloody oranges, please'.

Once or twice during the early summer we went for picnics in Kew Gardens. Kurt, Inge's fiancé, whom I liked very much, was usually in the family party. They were enjoyable outings and I still recall the sense of wonder I felt at my first visits to the tropical conservatories and steaming jungle houses. Enthusiastic descriptions were sent home and answers came back, pleased that we had somewhere to let off steam, since the *Gerresheimer Schweiz* was no longer available.

'When we come to London you will have to show us these wonders,' they wrote.

But these cheerful letters to Lotte and me, although they did not conceal how my parents felt their separation from us, did not dwell on the difficulties they were encountering in their efforts to follow us to Britain. In fact, they assured us constantly that it would not be long, that they were hopeful and longing to be with us again. Something of their difficulties and delays, however, emerges in other letters addressed to my relatives at about the same time.

Reading them one has the impression of my father as hurrying from one office or consulate to another, seeing people off at stations (promising to attend to all the things they had been obliged to leave undone), sorting belongings, parcelling up crates and bundles to be sent to Lotte and me, and dealing with the forced sale of the house and the consequent move to the attic flat. But his letters to my relations do not hint at the hardships that were invading daily life. The denial of ration-cards, the difficulty of finding shops that still served Jews, the obligation to wear a yellow star and be marked as *vogelfrei* (outlaws, without any protection from the law), the ever-present possibility of a repetition of the *Kristallnacht* pogrom and the physical risk involved in every excursion out of doors – these are never mentioned.

On 6 May my father wrote:

As for us, I am awaiting official confirmation from Bloomsbury House that the permit has been reinstated with the Home Office, or if not, I am hoping that a new one will be issued. Only then can I start dismantling our affairs here. . .

At Whitsun, 1939, he wrote:

Yesterday I accompanied the Lilienthals as far as Duisburg; they are emigrating to Holland. Mummy had a letter from Frau Heimbach, now in Brussels. . . I am at present sorting through my vast stamp collection in the hope that I may get permission to take these with me as 'Transfer of Goods', so that I could perhaps start a small philatelist business in the USA – probably the only thing a sixty-seven-year-old (as I shall be by then) will be able to do to keep his head above water. . .

And a note of bitter anxiety arising from the German regulation that only ten Marks could be taken out by refugees and from the British requirement for a guarantor:

. . .I am curious to see how the Home Office is going to decide in our case, since we have no guarantor. Our ten Marks won't last long: we should have to beg seven free suppers a week – Fridays with you?

15 May:

Today we got the papers for the sale of the house. Now I must see if the authorities will give us permission to maintain ourselves here; and to try and reach an agreement with the new owner to allow us to remain here until we can join you. That is going to be difficult. . .

This letter refers to the sale of our house to a party member, under duress, and for a fraction of its real value. In fact, the new owner did not allow my parents to remain and they had to move into the attic flat (for which they had to pay him rent). That was a time-consuming and exhausting business, just when they wanted to concentrate all their energies on arranging their escape. But still the cheerful letters came to us. Early in June my mother wrote:

Another week has gone and it seems such a long time since the train took you away. But now you'll feel like real English girls. Has your spoken English made any progress? Which school have you been registered with? Perhaps you will already have started school? I am longing to hear. Now you will be needing your last school reports; Daddy will find it hard to part with them. . . [My parents appear to have assumed that an English school would be eager to see our German school reports.]
    Continued on Sunday – *Prima*! Just now a letter arrived from England and it is the usual picture here: we sit round the breakfast-table, all ears, while Daddy reads your letters aloud. It always makes us all so happy. . . It is very disappointing that the school would not accept the children. Adolf says that the children *have* copies of the school reports. Don't they help?. . . School lasts from 9 o'clock till 4? Can that be right? How can one stand such a long day?
    At the moment I am trying to decide what to do with our furniture. We want to take only the absolute necessities. . .

Some days later:

I hear that you are washing your own things, dear Hannele. I'd like to see that picture! Is the washing really clean? And *prima* darning too! What a capable daughter I do have! Have you given a demonstration yet of how, in a flash, you are able to fabricate a complete dress, ready to wear? Approximately one hour, isn't it?
Continued Sunday: In the meantime your fervently awaited letters fluttered in. How interesting, dear Hannele, was your

description of the Strand. I too imagined it to be like the Rhine-meadows at Oberkassel. It was nice that Ala was your cavalier. I hope his heart won't play him any more tricks. [Ala had had a mild heart-attack.]

And now you have at last been registered with a school and tomorrow is going to be your first schoolday. I wonder if there will be any other emigrant children there. I can't tell you how eager I am for your news. And you write that such a lot of sport is practised. That will suit you fine, and you won't have to do much talking for that. Do you always have to wear a hat for sport? I hope that neither of you, in particular Hannele, will give Tante Rosel any trouble concerning what you wear, and that you will do what she says without argument.

Today I too enrolled at school – for a course in bakery, which is to begin next week. . . Frau Portens, the baker's wife, has had a son, weighing 8 lbs . . .

But all reports about me from Hampstead were not so favourable, judging from my father's reproving lecture (typed), which came soon after the shopping expedition to Kilburn, and which, I remember, upset me dreadfully.

My dear Hannele,

What I am writing today is to be a little conversation between father and daughter, not a rebuke, much less a scolding letter. Our upbringing of you stopped on the third of May. You have learnt at home the difference between right and wrong, between duty and pleasure, even if *we* were not always as strict about these things as we might have been; even if *you* yourselves were not always as particular about doing your duty or the right thing as you should have been. But we have confidence in you precisely because we have had proof again and again (Ohligs, holidays away, on visits, etc.) that you two *knew* how to behave correctly.

Now you may be away from us for years, perhaps for ever, (in your own home, I mean). Now we shall see whether the seeds that we have sown in deep love will grow and bear fruit. Just because you are at present with relatives, and just because it is Tante Rosel – that dear, over-burdened woman – who has taken on mother's role towards you, you must let *her* have the benefit of what you learnt at home, even if you have not always practised it there. You do see that, don't you?

When a woman like Tante Rosel, in her experience and affection, gives you an instruction, it should be a pleasure for you to carry it out. If you feel you can't do it just then, or that you would rather do it another way, then ask about it. But, for heaven's sake, don't do it in a truculent way, with a sulky face, as you have so often done here! 'He who wants to command must first learn to obey.'

This is *one* aspect of learning to fit in. The other is probably even more important to you: you are quite exceptionally anxious for affection, but you are also rather more concerned for your own advantage than I like. Do you really think it *is* to your advantage when you try to get your own way at all costs? All it really does, is to upset the people around you and in time destroy their affection for you (in part). I know myself, dear Hannele, that it is not easy to cure one's bad habits *oneself*, but if you can't do it, then it's you that will suffer most, just because you have such a soft little heart. For if you upset Tante Rosel and make her unhappy, then you give us too pain and worry – and we have quite enough of that here.

You must instead try and become Tante Rosel's friend, to support her in her troubles, and in turn you will be able to confide your problems and joys to her. And now, my dearest child – it wasn't a conversation after all, was it? For that two are needed. But as I was writing this, I saw you standing by my desk, tears running down your cheeks, saying to me, 'I really *will* try *very hard* to do better, so that Daddy doesn't have to send me any more letters like this one in a hurry.' That's right, isn't it, my dear child?

I wept buckets and swore to myself that I would reform.

Then followed the saga of the crate. For weeks my parents had been trying to get permission to send on the single consignment of used clothing and effects that was permitted to refugees. This involved repeated journeys to offices in Düsseldorf, but at last on 14 June my father wrote:

We have been toiling hard all day, since we have at last managed to get permission to send your things through the firm of Schenker & Co. We are not allowed to send anything new, so there should be no customs charges. Everything has been paid for at this end, you will only have to see to the transportation from the customs shed to your flat. We are not allowed to send the beds or bedding.

We have had a trial run at home today at packing and unpacking everything, since we are going to have to do it all over again at the customs shed here. There was not room for everything in the crate, so I have devised an ingenious bundle – everything is wrapped up and sewn into a waterproof cloth. . .

And:

At last the crate is off. It gave us a lot of trouble. At the customs shed we had to take everything out again, and everything that had been so carefully packed got into a terrible muddle. I hope it will arrive safely and that you don't have the same bother at your end. There is no reason why you should, as everything is worn and used – there is nothing new. We included some books and toys. . . We are concerned that the children should preserve their new clothes when the crate arrives and wear their old ones, since we shall not be able to buy new things in the foreseeable future.

My mother added:

The two dolls should please the girls particularly. Daddy had to pay five Marks to have them repaired. Hannele's has a new wig and new eyes. . . Daddy says you are not to quarrel when unpacking. . . I have enclosed some remnants. They are for mending your dresses, *not* for making doll's clothes! Keep your things tidy and help Tante Rosel to put everything away; I don't want her to have more extra work.

The doll's cot is for both of you and, of course, the doll's house. Take great care of that. Daddy says that it is something that can be handed down through the family; it is unique and your or Inge's children will also be able to have fun with it. . .

On 22 June my mother wrote delightedly:

That was a great joy for me on Mothering Sunday when your letters arrived with Hannele's lovely poems and Lotte's painting. I thank you, my dear children, for making it a happy day for me, and I am thoroughly proud of my two brats. Your picture, dear Lotte, I have hung up above the sofa; you really took a great deal of trouble over it. . .

I am glad to hear that you are both still eating so well: what a rich breakfast you have! [Eggs and bacon?] You seem at last to have learnt to take milk in your tea. Is there no coffee in England? What will Daddy do?. . .

I can hardly wait to hear all you are going to tell me about school. Will you really be wearing school uniform? I expect your hair is wild by now and in need of washing? Do most of the children in England also have a bob? The young *Backfische* tend to wear their hair in a 'Mozart-tail' tied with a pretty bow. . . [*Backfische*: Literally 'baked fish', and meaning, roughly speaking, 'teenager'.

Just for a change Daddy is not at home and there is no one here now to ask anxiously, 'When is Daddy coming home?'. . . No news from Walter; our patience is being put to a severe test. . .

My mother is referring to her brother, Walter, the sabre-scarred 'race-desecrator', who had fled to Czechoslovakia in 1937. He had vanished when the Germans marched in. My parents had feared the worst and their letters continually mentioned their anxiety, but in her next letter my mother wrote:

First I want to let you know that we have at last had a letter from Walter himself, from the prison at Dresden. He writes that they have enough to eat and are being treated well. You can imagine the joy to see his handwriting again after such a long time. Perhaps you heard the sound of the heavy weight dropping off our chests, even over there. He belatedly congratulated us all on our birthdays: me, Oma, Rosel and Egon – he hasn't forgotten anyone.

My mother was so relieved to know that her brother was alive and, from his own account, well-treated, even though he had been recaptured and brought back to a German prison. She did not yet know the new 'Justice' of the Third Reich. Years later we discovered that after a lengthy imprisonment Walter was transferred to a Munich prison to await his trial. He was found guilty of *Rassenschande* and beheaded with an axe.

My mother was very concerned that we should not spoil our good clothes before going to America, and anxious that our crate should arrive:

> I do hope you won't have to purchase a wardrobe to store the contents of the crate. If you feel you can do without some of the things, dear Rosel, you can give them away. In general though, most of the things are still wearable by the children, otherwise they'll soon have nothing decent left and we really shan't be able to buy them new clothes out there. They have been able to prance around in their new things until now and it won't do them any harm to wear an old coat now. . . A lot of things could be stored in their cases, perhaps those things that should be kept for later. You do understand, dear Rosel, that the children have to keep some things decent for going to America? That's why I have sent so many of their older clothes. . . We are overjoyed at the prospect of the new permit. Daddy will write more about this.

But the crate was a long time coming and she became worried:

> And now the question of whether your crate and bundle were still waiting at the customs office or got burnt at the depot. We calculated that to replace all the things would cost at least 500 Marks: there was bed-linen and towels, woollen dresses and winter underwear, three very good winter coats and two older ones, jumpers (including your beloved red one, dear Hannele), dolls, books and, of course, the lovely Bavarian doll's house. We shall have to wait and see. Meantime we read in the papers that a large warehouse got burnt down, and Lotte mentioned in her letter that you were going to visit the roof-garden of one, and so I got scared. [My mother confused 'warehouse' and 'store'. We were probably going to visit the roof-garden at Derry and Toms.] But I think it must have been the day you were going to the zoo.

Lehrer Zürndorfer and his children, Hugo, Max, Rosel and Adolf

My father as a young man, 1899

My mother (left) and her sister

Karl Röttger with his children and me (middle)

Proud father, 1933, the year Hitler came to power

Me in my favourite coat

Anna the maid, Lotte and me in *Fasching* costume

My first schoolday, 8 April 1932, with customary *Schultüte* (horn of sweets)

Lotte's first schoolday, 1936, inscribed 'the two scholars' by my father

'Auntie' – Mary Salmon

Kathleen Salmon

My maternal grandparents, who had been badly shocked by the pogroms and had come to stay at Gerresheim, had to return home. My mother wondered if she would ever see them again, for her departure for England and America seemed imminent. But there was some distraction from painful leavetaking:

My dear Mama did not have much time to give way to the pain of parting, which was good, although during the past few days I have been rather irritated by her. I will give you an account of what they have done with all the junk stored for more than ten years in our cellars.

First Papa brought the pieces of furniture (all thick with dust) into the yard and Mama washed them down with soap-suds, till they looked a little more presentable. Then they were placed in an empty room in the hope that they would bring in a few Marks, Papa calculated roughly 100 Marks. My remarks about 'old junk' were rejected with disdain, and Mama went on sorting what amounted to old rags. I found amongst them things that brought back my girlhood, indeed, my childhood. After the best of these had been solemnly arranged, Adolf and I fetched the second-hand dealers from the *Altstadt*, some of whom fled in horror without making an offer, others offered ten Marks for the lot, including three paintings. At long last my dear Papa had to concede, after a bitter struggle, that his hopes of 'riches' had come to nothing.

Her last three days here, my dear Mama spent in re-sorting her rubbish. She would not have devoted as much time to packing her bed-linen, her porcelain and china, as to these few old rags. Quite exhausted we at last took them to the station. I hope Mama won't have done herself any harm with all her grubbing about. The 'battlefield' remained behind for us: the old pieces of furniture are still lying around.

You, my dear Hannele, can understand only too well how hard it is to part with old rags, but I believe if you had seen how such things can accumulate, it would have cured you of your mania. And now *Pappile* [daddy] is sitting disconsolately at his corner desk, starting to tear up with a heavy heart his high-stacked correspondence of the last fifty years! Up to now I haven't noticed much difference. And if I ask him, 'What are you going to do with this or that magazine, such as the *Literary Echo* or *Theatre World*?' then I get the answer, 'That I am taking with me, of course.' My hair stands on end, each one separately, at the thought. Yes, my dear children, you have inherited this trait from two sides of the family: from my mother and your father!

At some stage we must have sent a photo of ourselves at long last, in answer to their repeated pleadings for one:

In front of me is your magnificent photograph, my dear children, and I can't get my fill of looking [writes my mother]. I almost feel that you are there, and about to start talking any minute . . . I can see how your cheeks have filled out and particularly noticeable, my dear Hannele, is your bosom: it has grown, quite distinctly! And Lotte's legs – do they only seem to be fatter, or are they so indeed? Daddy shows the photos to anyone who comes across his path, naturally with great pride. There now, don't start getting conceited.

There was more news of my friend, Inge Lewin, who had been at the station at Rotterdam. In May my father had written that she and her mother and sisters were 'on high seas on their way to join their father in Havana'. But now, in July, he wrote of the failure of their attempt.

Yesterday we received a card from Amsterdam from Frau Lewin. They must have undergone a great deal of hardship, particularly on their return journey. For about six weeks they were continuously at sea. Herr Lewin went every day six or seven times in a small boat from Havana to the side of the ship; he was able to see them and talk to his wife and children, but he was not able to kiss and hug them. They were not allowed to land, but were taken back to Holland. Inge would like your address which I shall send tomorrow. Frau Lewin hopes that Inge and her sister will soon be able to attend school. At present they are in quarantine . . . I have no idea what finally happened to Inge and her family.

On 5 July my father wrote:

My dear Children – This is the first time in nine weeks since your departure, that we have had no news from you for a whole week. Mummy, who is still at her bakery course, which lasts five hours and tires her very much, is feeling very anxious. [Later she also took courses in hairdressing, catering, massage, as well as English, hoping to be able to use one or other of these skills in America to bring in some money.] I hope the post will bring something tomorrow. I hope all is well at Belsize Square? How is Ala? . . . Have crate and bundle not arrived yet?

The crate did arrive. Apparently my aunt failed to understand that it must be collected from the customs shed, and so storage charges were incurred. This vexed my father, as he had tried to spare them all expense. But when the large wooden crate and bundle finally appeared before us, we unpacked it excitely in the presence of all my 'aaahing' and 'uuuhing' relatives; it was like a hundred birthdays wrapped into one. From their depths we drew many old and loved friends. Hidden in a doll's house chest I found my little gold ring with the tiny ruby, which my father would not let me take on the journey in case of trouble. There were splendid presents for my relatives: a special canteen of silver cutlery for my cousin's wedding (whenever that might be) and enough bed-linen to last for years.

We had started school in the second week of June, just a few weeks before the summer holidays. Our days there are a complete blur to me. I have no recollection now of the other children, the lessons, the teachers, classrooms or playground. It was like being a deaf-mute in a busy crowd. There was the complete lack of language, and too many changes had followed each other too fast. It was like living behind a thick curtain that muffled everything.

One day in the hall during assembly a teacher was reading to us and a word shot across the babble of sounds and hit me: 'Nebuchadnezzar'! It was the same in German. Wasn't he the man who had lived for hundreds of years? I felt overjoyed; I knew what they were talking about! And for the whole of that assembly my mind played around that biblical name and I stayed alert in case I could invest some other word with meaning.

I believe from that point on I started picking up words here and there from public utterance and understanding them. I was being assimilated.

Once they had had our letters reporting our first experiences at school, my mother's questions and comments arrived:

> I am so glad that you are with children of your own age . . . It will take a while before all the different subjects no longer seem like double Dutch to you.
> We were very amused by Hannele's account of her first swimming attempts – it made us laugh a great deal. Next time it will be easier, never fear . . .
> I think your school lunches make a good midday meal. Next time you must send me the recipe for your cake in German, dear Hannele. What weight is that 'four ounzes [sic] flour'?

From now on my parents were clearly making every effort to speed up their preparations for emigration, but they were sadly distracted by the enforced change of flat:

> I am beginning to feel glum about our move [wrote my mother]. We've had the carpenter here to alter and repair some of the furniture that we want to take with us when we emigrate. We only want to take the *Biedermeier* desk and matching cupboard, the oval table with matching chairs and a small walnut sideboard. He is going to convert our heavy beds into sofa-beds and he is also going to reduce the tall wardrobes. I am wondering how it will all turn out. Perhaps it *would* be wisest for us to buy some furniture in your markets, but without money one can't buy furniture, not even in England!

A fortnight later my mother wrote:

> Our hopes to be with you soon look very grey; we don't even know yet whether it will be permitted at all for us to come via England . . . in the meantime the enforced removal is drawing near – and I am not looking forward one bit, even though it is only two flights up . . .

My father wrote: [18 July]

> Four to five hours are spent in town every day, rushing now here, now there. Life insurance, visiting the Heilbronners, the Bergs, Fleischhackers, the Jewish community – all of them

want help and advice. And then there is the now ludicrously large correspondence to deal with . . . On Monday I received the following astonishing letter from the Jewish Aid Committee in London:

'Dear Sir,

With reference to your desire to enter this country, we would inform you that an application on your behalf has been lodged with the Home Office. As soon as we hear from them we shall notify you accordingly.

Yours faithfully,
A. Closs (Immigration Dept.)'

I call this letter 'astonishing', because it arrived almost *three* months after the Committee sent me a telegram stating: 'Permit Granted' . . .

So their hopes were crushed once more. Through some muddle in London they were back where they had started and three precious months were wasted. This note was, in fact, the first communication my father had received from the hard-pressed Committee since his original application for an entry permit more than *six* months earlier, when he had hoped we could all leave together. 'It is lucky,' he wrote, 'that neither Else nor I are infected by the general nervousness that is experienced by most of the people who are waiting to leave, as we are.'

My relatives tried to convince him that everything would work out once they got to England, and that they too could come to Belsize Square for a start. But my father was adamant that he would not be a liability: 'We *cannot* also land on you. Haven't you got enough with our brats?'

At length the new permit was issued, distinguished from the first only by a different number. Its final reception galvanized my father. On 1 August he wrote:

Today I went to Cologne to the Emigration authorities (that is the prescribed procedure for emigration). I have ordered our passports. I then went to the British Consulate and showed them the permit and received two questionnaires. I am to return these only when I have the passports, which, according to my reckoning will take five to six weeks. Now that I have the permit I am going to pursue the matter energetically, but without panic . . . When I got home last night, Else was still reading the children's birthday letters, glowing all over, but I am afraid that during the next few days her glow will die away, because on Thursday we have to move to the flat upstairs.

On 3 August:

Four months ago today, dear children, you went out into the world. A propos of this occasion we too are moving today. We are now eight metres nearer heaven. I think all of us are going to feel enormously stiff tomorrow: Mummy, Frau Ortmann (who came to help) and I also, since I must have gone up the twenty stairs about seventy times, heavily laden. We now have to take the whole flat again and pay for it too.

On 8 August:

Since my time will shortly be taken up with continuous negotiations for several weeks to come: authorities, consulate etc., I want to use this evening to answer your wonderful letters for my birthday. Even if it is not pedagogic to say so, I must admit that Hannele has hit the jackpot with her sixty-five candles and all the decorations and her poem and long letter. Lotte's jackpot is almost as big in her bright description of her own magnificent birthday, so that I have to admit you would not have been able to celebrate your birthday so well here, since there are not many friends or relatives left.

But a new obstacle was contributed by the German Passport Office, for on 9 August my father wrote:

As for our emigration business: tomorrow I shall have to start from scratch all over again. The office at Cologne drew up our forms in the name of *Zwi*dorf, instead of *Zürn*dorf, and so I had to go to Cologne again today to the passport office and start again . . . When one reads the papers today one finds it hard to retain the hope that peace can be maintained much longer . . . I now have another appointment for 22 August, and I must somehow obtain 'declarations of good intent' from Walter and Max by then . . . Else is now busy with a course in confectionery & praline-making.

15 August:

On Tuesday 22 August we have been summoned to the passport office. If only we can manage to get our three declarations of good intent by then . . .

But now, on top of everything else, they had news that Uncle Ala had suffered another heart-attack, followed by a stroke.

If there is an opportunity I shall ask if I can get a temporary passport to visit you briefly on account of Ala's serious illness. Be nice and quiet, children, and be careful what you eat and drink in this hot weather . . . We are very concerned about Ala's illness.

When I read that I wished so terribly that both he and Mummy might come, and then we could simply keep them here.

[My mother added:] I am worried, dear Rosel, about how you are going to cope with all this extra work, since Ala now needs careful nursing. I do hope the children will be a real help. They can wash up and wipe: Hannele likes peeling potatoes and is good at dusting and sweeping . . .

On 17 August my father wrote:

The evening post has been, without bringing any news from you. In thought we are with you, particularly in the mornings when you get in touch with the hospital to enquire after Ala's night. It is a torture to me to be so powerless to help . . .

At present I am spending two to three hours every morning with the authorities and things are progressing quite nicely. Tomorrow we are having our passport photos taken, so that they are ready when needed. Mummy went to the dentist today to get the most necessary work done before we go. I shall also send her to Professor Baden, the intestine specialist . . .

A day later he wrote:

Since our telephone call to you we have written one letter and three cards. Have they arrived? One must not be impatient just now, since everything seems to be taking much longer than usual. We still hope sincerely that peace will last, in which case we might be with you in three to four weeks . . .

In the middle of the summer holidays the authorities notified my aunt that as part of the scheme to evacuate London of children, our school was being sent to Rickmansworth in Hertfordshire.

When the day came we all had to form into lines in the playground, wearing school hats, labelled once more like parcels being sent off by post. Here we were being uprooted again, after only a few months in Hampstead. With hugs and kisses we took tearful leave of our aunt and cousins on the station platform, before being bustled into the compartment.

The train was full of children in navy tunics and white blouses, carrying bundles and bags and sandwich-packs and those buff, always-in-the-way gasmask boxes. I was quite unable to anticipate what lay in store for us, not knowing anything of English home life. It had been impressed on me, however, by my worried aunt to make sure that Lotte and I stayed together. I was by now thirteen and Lotte was ten.

Miss Ping, our headmistress, was in charge. She was a gentle, grey-haired woman with very pink cheeks. She was a kind person and, so far as her responsibilities allowed, she tried to keep an eye on Lotte and me, having promised my aunt to see that we did not get separated.

As we spilled out of the train at Rickmansworth after little over an hour's ride, open lorries were waiting for us. We were divided up into different lorry loads, each one to go to a different street. Ours took us to the new estate. We were unloaded on to a street of carrot-red houses with tiny front gardens in which the housewives were already gathering in sympathetic and curious knots, no doubt discussing the tribulation that was being visited on them. Lotte and I clung together like waifs in a Victorian painting.

10 Evacuees

Luckily it was a fine day, for we had to stay where we had been unloaded and wait until we were selected by our prospective foster mothers. It was very much like a street market: we were there for inspection, but instead of choosing firm, ripe tomatoes, the women were looking for nice, clean, and preferably pretty children. The housewives issued forth, some hurrying to get the best bargains. They looked us over, asked us questions, consulted the teacher in charge of the consignment, and finally made their choice and went off with a timid, or intrepid evacuee in tow.

At first it seemed like an adventure: all of us were sharing in it and it was fun to watch other children being marched off. 'Poor Jean, her woman looks very strict.' Jimmy, the class entertainer, danced along behind his 'lady', turning back to us every so often, clowning bravely, until told to come to heel. Ruth went off broadly grinning with her foster mother, a large, jolly woman, who was being tugged along by a large, bouncing dog.

We appraised our prospective foster guardians as critically as they did us, and each departure of a pupil was commented on by those of us who were left. On several occasions someone asked for Lotte, who looked very appealing with her enormous brown eyes and dark curls. But true to our promise we clung together like saplings on an exposed heath and in my very best foreign accent I said staunchly, 'Vee are togezzer,' whereupon the 'buyer' moved on hastily to inspect more reliable British goods. On several occasions the teacher spoke to some lady, looking at us, hoping to get us placed. But the fact that we were not merely evacuees, but also German refugees was disconcerting, particularly as there were two of us, one wispy and delicate, the other lanky with a shock of bushy hair. The teacher thought we might have to be prepared to be separated after all, if someone didn't come for us soon. That was unthinkable. Tears were beginning to form in Lotte's eyes, and I too was feeling dejected.

Then a very cheerful-looking girl appeared and asked for Lotte. I told her that we were 'togezzer' and the teacher explained it all to her. The young girl said that she was not there to select evacuees for herself, but for a neighbour who couldn't come, and she supposed there would be room for the two of us. 'I don't know what Mrs H will say, but I expect it will be all right. Come along then.'

She took us along to her home, gave us tea and chatted cheerfully to us all the time, until it was time for the neighbour to have returned.

The recollection I have is that when the door opened in response to the girl's knock, a skinny little witch-woman with a long red nose looked at us from bulging, red-rimmed eyes with unconcealed horror. She had not bargained for *two* evacuees and when she was informed that we were refugees, *German* refugees, she did not conceal her disapproval. The girl apologized in embarrassment, for this conversation took place in front of us, and – though I did not understand every word – the gist was clear enough. The girl had obviously acted from a sympathetic impulse, but had exceeded her brief. She bade us farewell as encouragingly as she could, nevertheless glad to be out of it. When she left us with Mrs H we felt quite deserted, as though we had lost the last friend we had.

As we crossed the threshold, fully aware that we were unwelcome, a sense of claustrophobia enveloped me. Was this to be our life from now on? How did one deal with it all? Mrs H regarded us suspiciously.

'You'll have to come in for tonight, I suppose,' she said grudgingly.

She had wispy grey hair and false teeth that were too big and made her look like *Kasperle*, the German Punch whom I had seen at the fairs on the Rhine-meadows. I felt utterly bewildered and miserable. We could run away, I thought, back to London, if life became too impossible. But I knew very well that we would not be allowed to remain there, and that Tante Rosel had enough problems and worries already, with my uncle ill, perhaps dying, and that we could not add to them.

Then Mr H came home and after a loudly whispered conversation with his wife, he told us to stand in front of him. He then started bombarding us with searching questions about Germany. Under this stern interrogation, with our stammered attempts at answers being treated with great suspicion as the cunning vacillations of the enemy aliens, we felt very alien indeed. They grew impatient and shouted louder and louder at us. When this produced no more satisfactory results, we got only sullen and suspicious looks and snapped orders.

High tea that first day there was a very miserable affair. The food was very different from what we had been used to. I think there were little sausages on toast, but all the tension and unhappiness of the past hour had driven my appetite away; I felt choked and simply could not force down the sausage or the toast, both of which were swimming with grease. Then they got very cross about that and gave me a long lecture of which I understood very little except disapproval.

At last it was bedtime and we could escape to the tiny room in which there was space only for a single bed and a narrow chest. We were very tired that night and though it was very uncomfortable lying stiffly side by side in the single bed, we cried ourselves to sleep.

I believe Mrs H went 'to see about it' in the morning, but the WVS explained that there simply was no other vacancy just then, and that they would have to put up with us. They were given money for the two of us and extra money with which to buy another bed. They probably decided to make the best of it and treat us as one. The second bed was always promised, but never came and we continued to sleep badly in that narrow space, with the blankets never covering both of us, so that we decided to try sleeping foot to head. It was better. When that was discovered the next morning, however, we were shouted at for doing such a 'scandalous thing'.

It was the beginning of furtiveness on our part, because we continued to sleep head to foot – any other way was impossible – but we took the precaution of starting off side by side and quickly changing back early in the morning before she came to wake us. It meant that we had to be careful not to oversleep.

Teatime, when everyone was home, was a hated meal. Once a postcard had arrived from Tante Rosel, written in German, and Mr H confiscated the card without letting us see it. He wasn't going to have anything of this sort in his house! How did he know we weren't spies? I suppose he thought that if German paratroopers could disguise themselves as nuns – as they were then rumoured to do – a team of dwarf spies might be disguised as children. At any rate, he continued quizzing us whenever we were in his presence, taking great care not to discuss anything to do with the war in front of us. There was no one to turn to. This new life was frightening and miserable and I felt trapped.

Gladys H, conscious of her superiority as a true-born Briton and the daughter of the house, and three years older than me, shared her parents' suspicions and spoke to me only to issue peremptory instructions. If I failed to understand, or tried to answer back, stumbling over the English words, she would put her hands on her hips in a pose of exasperation and shout, 'Don't *arg*ue, don't *arg*ue – you are always *arg*uing!'

For a long time I could not make out what the word 'argue', which always occurred in a different context, meant. When I tried to ask, Gladys would only shout 'Don't *arg*ue,' even louder. I can remember nothing else about her except that on Saturday mornings she always rushed out to the baker's van and held long conversations with the baker's boy, always smiling and sweet. One Saturday Lotte and I saw her bottom sticking out of the van for a long time and when we passed by downstairs we realized that she was actually *kissing* him! It was our turn to be scandalized. Gladys was a lost woman in our eyes, for our Gerresheim upbringing, and perhaps the isolation of the last years, had left us very naïve.

A new anxiety arose when, in the atmosphere of suspicion and dislike that surrounded us, I became tense and prone to wetting my pants. Once before at the age of seven some emotional strain had caused me to start wetting my bed for a short period while on holiday. Now I was terrified in case I should also wet the bed, and often forced myself to stay awake in case I should be tricked, by a dream perhaps, into error while I slept. The pants were bad enough! I could not face the prospect of Mrs H's knowing. I felt very ashamed too and was at my wits' end as to how to deal with this.

I couldn't give her my pants to wash, for then she would find out. I couldn't bring myself to tell her that I occasionally suffered from a weak bladder; I could imagine her scorn and horror. So, feeling guilty, I used to scurry into the bathroom with my thick woolly knickers to wash them out. Drying them was a worse problem. The logical thing would have been to face Mrs H and tell her that I preferred to see to my own pants, but the logical thing might not have worked in that house; besides, I felt too embarrassed. The drying of the pants became for me a problem of enormous proportions. I would wring them out after washing and hide them until bedtime, when I could drape them all over the bedstead. They were still damp in the morning and this meant hiding them away again until the next night. They were still damp when I put them on again, and that can hardly have helped the original trouble. All this subterfuge weighed heavily and made my crime all the more shameful to me.

One Saturday, when I was locked in the bathroom with my pants, someone tried the door. Then Mrs H started hammering and shouting, 'What are you doing in there? Why have you locked the door?'

Silence.

'You secretive little thing, let me in at once, or I'll call the police!'

I don't know if she thought I was sending messages to the German High Command through the bathroom drains, but I was paralysed with fear and just stood there. I think if I could have flushed myself down the lavatory, I would have done so. Mrs H went on shouting and hammering, becoming more and more hysterical. At last I steeled myself to open the door and explain.

She burst in and looked all round. I don't know what she was looking for. I think she felt disappointed at finding nothing more than home laundry, although she seemed amazed at the number of pairs of pants by which I was surrounded. I tried to explain, but she clearly thought I was a mental case to have 'accidents' at my age. From then on the coldness towards me became arctic, and I think it was only the daily escape to school that kept me sane.

Quite soon after being billeted with Mrs H, Inge visited us with Mrs Ettinghausen, our sponsor. I don't know if this did anything to allay the suspicions of Mrs H, but it certainly cheered us up. Eagerly we asked for news of our parents' coming. The letters from Düsseldorf that Inge brought told not only of their preparations, but also of new difficulties:

> Mummy is working hard making lists and I have to go once more to the passport office tomorrow, but the English Consulate in Cologne has, as I heard today, stopped working for the time being. Unless we have a visa, our passports are of little use. We must simply keep hoping, and in good spirits . . .

But the main news that Inge had for us was about Uncle Ala, who was by now very ill. Several times during her visit I was on the point of begging her to take us back to Hampstead, but of course I knew that wouldn't do. It was quite a wrench to see her off at the station.

A little later Inge came again, with Egon. This time it was to tell us of Ala's death.

There were more letters from home:

> Today I sent off a long letter to you . . . I can only say that *we* are doing everything possible to speed our going. We too are longing to see you. Some precious time was lost through the move, but pray to God that peace remains, because then that lost time can easily be made up. It is nine o'clock Saturday evening. I am just about to go to the Bergs to listen to the wireless . . .

The war was little more than a week away.

11 Outbreak of War

At first the local school bewildered me. The boys seemed very rough; the headmaster actually caned them across the backside. Girls too were caned, though usually by the assistant head-mistress. I was terrified of being caned: it looked painful and undignified. But my general memory of that school is a happy one. I think the teachers must have taken a great deal of trouble and tried to encourage me. Somehow my English must have improved quite quickly. I don't know at what point it became my 'first' language. I continued to write poems, diaries and letters to relatives in German. For some time Lotte and I continued to speak in German when alone together, for I felt that German was a link betwen my parents and us. It was the language of our lives together and I felt in some indefinable way disloyal at abandoning its use altogether. But we heard only English spoken and it became a necessity for survival. Gradually Lotte and I started conversing in a hotchpotch of English and German, but quite soon English became our spoken language, and I remember waking one night and realizing that I had been dreaming in English.

Some of my teachers took pains to help me with my grammar: prepositions and word order were the main stumbling blocks. Mr Menzies, the geography teacher, in particular was conscientious and helped me a lot. He was a very upright, grave man who always wore a neatly pressed suit. I stood a little in awe of him and felt I was not managing his subject at all, because my written work always came back crawling with corrections in crimson ink. In fact, most of the corrections were linguistic and I was always expected to do corrections.

Pronunciation was by far the highest hurdle: I lisped my 'ths' and rasped my 'rs' and inverted my 'ws' and 'vs'. I remember how one teacher took a sadistic delight in making me repeat 'trigonometry' before the whole class. Everyone roared at my 'tchigenometchy' (to get the right effect 'ch' is pronounced as in 'loch'). Luckily I didn't mind being laughed at and quite enjoyed being the focus of attention, for there was no malice or derision in the laughter. The children were all very friendly and helpful.

Miss Milsom I remember very clearly. She was so pretty, with loose fair hair and very blue eyes that crinkled up when she smiled. She was both the gym mistress and singing teacher, as well as the deputy head in charge of girls. It was the songs she made us sing that established her as a romantic figure in my eyes, especially as we knew that her fiancé was in the forces and far away. Her face assumed a melancholy expression when she sang 'My Father He Hath Locked the Door, My Mother Keeps the Key' or 'Where'er You Walk'. She used to appear in very short, prettily tailored gym-slips and leapt lightly about as she issued orders in firm, ringing tones, constantly blowing her whistle at our clumsy responses. She was always very kind to me.

Perhaps my romantic crushes, which came and went like a rash of measles, may have helped me in those puzzling days of insecurity. At this school, for some reason now inexplicable to me, the little Welsh maths teacher, Mr Rowlands, aroused in me a turmoil of adoration and desire to please (which was, of course, an excellent incentive for my maths). He was young, single, vivacious and devoted to his subject, a subject that had hitherto appeared to me like a field of thistles and needed wary walking.

He felt very strongly that we who were in the 'Remove' (the class of boys and girls due to leave school at the end of the next summer term, at fourteen) were most ill-equipped in the mathematical accomplishments. The school curriculum didn't require higher mathematical skills, but those of us who wanted to better ourselves, he told us, could come to him after school for extra lessons in algebra, logarithms and trigonometry and do extra homework.

My father would have marvelled to see me one of the first to clamour for extra lessons. I convinced myself that I wanted to improve my knowledge of the subject, whereas if truth were to be faced, I only wanted to prolong the hour of contact with him.

Ruth Meyer, another refugee-evacuee from Hampstead, with whom I became good friends, luckily caught the infection too, so that we had some very companionable hours discussing Mr Rowlands and singing his praises to each other.

A novelty of the English school was organized games. They had no place in German schools and I was certainly not very adept at them. I particularly remember netball as a muddly, confusing business, which sometimes meant staying after school for practice. In a way I quite enjoyed it, even succeeding in getting the ball through the net occasionally, but I never fully understood the different tasks of all the people milling about the court. The whistle was forever blowing, and I was always afraid of appearing at the wrong end of the court. It was quite different from *Völkerball* which I had played in the old days in Gerresheim, before the cars and before the Nazis.

In those days Rickmansworth was still a small country town: fields and woodland were not far away and the vast housing estates had not yet encroached on the countryside, and there were lovely walks to be had starting not far beyond the back door. I used to go for long walks with Lotte or Ruth before school started again. It was a great comfort to get away from the constricting atmosphere of our billet. Ruth had been placed with the jolly woman with the large dog. She was in her thirties and childless, and as her husband was often away on business she was glad of Ruth's company and treated her like a daughter. She was a warm-hearted, motherly person, always roaring with laughter. Whenever I came round calling for Ruth, she welcomed me warmly and commiserated with me for having struck unlucky with my lodgings. Any kindness was balm. The similarity of background had drawn Ruth and me together and she became an intimate friend to whom I could unburden myself.

There was much talk of war. It must have been in late August when one hot day I lay in the dry grass at the edge of a cornfield. It felt so peaceful: the sky was very blue above and my eyes closed. I lay there half-dreaming, half-dozing, exulting like a cat in the warm sun. Larksongs were spiralling into the sky and butterflies drifted lightly on warm currents of air. I felt a deep content. I faintly heard a low buzz like a bee, then it seemed more like a hum high up. A small, silver bird glinted in the depth of blue. It looked very beautiful and the sound was soft and reassuring. I remember this moment so well, because it was the last time that I associated the drowsy hum of an aeroplane with summer ease and ripening corn. When the plane had quite gone and the sound died away, I suddenly felt a strange premonition of change, as though a lens had shifted slightly: the glint of the sun seemed sinister, the solitude like emptiness and the shadows between the trees assumed a menacing quality.

It wasn't long after that blissful summer's day that one Sunday morning Ruth and I went for a long walk through the rolling countryside above Rickmansworth. Autumn was already touching the leaves. As adolescents will do, we talked about momentous things: life, death, and the future, which didn't look too bright. I was worried about leaving school so soon, completely untrained. I wanted to take the shorthand-typing classes, but they cost five shillings a week, and where was I going to get that from? My dreams of becoming a foreign correspondent faded.

But it was a lovely morning and we soon fell into a lighter vein. The sound of the church bells drifted up to us and we had worked up a great appetite. Just as we were turning back towards town, we heard a long, shrill, undulating wail. We started running back as fast as we could. We knew that the sirens were to be sounded for air-raids, because we had been told about it at school, but never before had we actually heard this lingering howl. When I arrived back at the house everyone was gathered around the wireless, listening with serious faces.

War had been declared. From the way Mrs H was carrying on it seemed as if death and damnation would rain from the skies at any moment. Of course, I thought at once of Mummy and Daddy. What would happen now? All communications between England and Germany had been stopped. How could they come to us now? It would, of course, have been quite impossible to voice any of these worries to our foster parents, who now regarded us with even greater disapproval and caution. It was an ambivalent position to be in, full of conflicting emotions.

England was now at war with Germany and patriotic feeling was inevitably strong, and we, trying to become one with our new surroundings, responded to it. The memory of the *Kristallnacht* and the terrors of our last months in Germany left us in no doubt who was the enemy. The Nazis had, after all, driven us from our home and our parents and destroyed everything. I hated the Nazis. But in my mind I still kept some distinction between the Nazis and the Germans. For, wasn't I German, weren't my parents German, weren't they in Germany and in danger from English bombs? Whenever, in the days to come, the news broadcasts spoke of victorious raids over Düsseldorf, the conflicting emotions sometimes became intolerable. I recall actually being aware of experiencing two distinct and contradictory emotions at one and the same time, and how I longed to be able to feel only one.

After that Sunday, 3 September 1939, I felt as if a play for which we had been rehearsing a long time was at last to be performed. There was sudden activity everywhere and a heightened tension. All sorts of plans were suddenly put into operation; people were more alive and much kinder to each other, as though it were Christmas. There was a sort of brotherliness, a drawing together, a sense of sharing. And I wanted desperately to be part of it. It was such a warming feeling, but often, when I felt most closely involved, I was reminded sharply of my alien position.

I remember how in those early days of war the long, brown-green camouflaged convoys passed through the High Street, tanks and lorries full of soldiers on their way to the coast. People used to rush out on the street, waving and shouting and encouraging the soldiers on their way. It is a comforting feeling to be part of a cheering crowd and one day Lotte and I too ran out and waved back to the soldiers, who were laughing and shouting and clowning about in the back of their lorries in their brand-new battledress.

Suddenly I heard a woman say to another, 'Look at those two little Germans. What are they doing here? The cheek of it, cheering *our* soldiers. It oughtn't to be allowed. It ought to be stopped!'

I had never felt so lonely in my life. My hand dropped, my cheers petered out and soon Lotte and I drifted away out of the crowd, back to the H's where we were regarded as intrusive, unwanted foreigners as well. I felt deeply troubled and it may well be that from those days stems my almost pathological reluctance to tell people where I was born. Even though we were gradually putting down roots in English soil, odd events or remarks would often rip them out again.

We did not have any news from home until several weeks after the outbreak of war. My parents had by then learnt of Ala's death and of our evacuation.

On 17 September my father wrote:

Dear All,

I am so terribly sorry for all of us that I can't be with you now, when the worries of those torn asunder are doubled and the possibilities of corresponding are diminished, and above all when all of us are saddened by the death of our dear Ala. If I could only be by your side now, dear Rosel, so that you could unload your grief for him on me; not even the children are with you now . . .

Twelve days have passed without any news from you and one can't help worrying about your situation. In order to keep this letter as short as possible I will confine myself to precise questions concerning the children and I beg you to address your letters to my friend Dr Martha Heymann-Frank, Brussels . . .

With the war letters could no longer come direct, but had to be sent by way of friends in Holland or Belgium – as yet unoccupied – and they took three to four weeks. To avoid overburdening friends – who were refugees themselves, without funds and often acting as postmasters for several families – the routes had to be varied and the number of letters restricted.

My father continued:

Please send this letter to the children, if possible, so that they can answer the following questions frankly. We also need to know if we can continue to write in German, or if we must write in your language . . .

Dear Children,

Write to us via Tante Rosel.

1) Are you well? Quite sure?
2) Are you together or separated?
3) Do you continue lessons with your old teachers?
4) Are you keeping cheerful? Children should be cheerful and happy, even if they have worries.
5) Are you kind to each other, or do you quarrel a lot?

On our account you may be *quite* reassured: we are well and always thinking of you. Only we are longing to see your handwriting again . . .

This letter, which told me that my parents were well, still planning to follow us, temporarily distracted me from the petty miseries of the H ménage, where we were unwanted and resented. I took refuge in the assurance of my parents' love and longing to be with us.

Hertfordshire was in the country and Rickmansworth in those days was about an hour's run from London, but whenever there was a raid on London the air-raid sirens would go automatically. Often we could see the planes, both going and returning, or at any rate, hear them. After a while most of us used to be able to recognize the German planes, just from the sound of the engines. How relieved we used to feel to hear the last of their engines die away and the sound of the All Clear.

Most people observed the air-raid drill and went into the shelters, and, if they had any, kept the black-out curtains firmly shut and took other needful precautions. But I don't think anyone went to quite such dramatic lengths as Mrs H.

One night – it must have been the first time the siren went at night – I was suddenly shaken out of sleep. Not being fully awake I was terrified out of my wits, for there by our bed stood a shape in a long white garment with grizzly hair falling over its shoulders, its haggard face grotesquely lit from below by the flickering flame of a candle, the mouth puckered and collapsed inwards, the eyes staring and glittering and a voice screeching, 'Get up! Get up, this instant and follow me!'

I felt sure I was dreaming; it was like one of Grimm's fairy tales. After some more fierce shaking, the bed-covers were pulled off us and, fully awakened by the chill air, I recognized the strident tones of Mrs H.

'What's the matter?' I kept asking, but in answer I had a rough sack pulled over my head, so that I couldn't see, and could barely breathe. Lotte was led out without a sack over her head, but I had to totter behind, as best as I could, following the glow of the candle, groping and stumbling. I lifted the sack off my face in order to see where I was going. Mrs H took us into her bedroom and told Lotte to get into bed with her and to hide herself deep under the bedclothes. I was pushed into a corner, barefoot on the cold lino, and told to kneel down and pray. I crouched there trembling with cold and fear. I heard the planes passing over.

'Pray!' she screamed, 'and pull that sack down!' She blew out the candle and there we were, punished in sackcloth and darkness for our sins. I did not realize that sacks had been issued in case of flying glass and an explanation would have helped. I was more upset by her strange, extreme behaviour than by the fear of bombs. Mr H was out with the home guard and Gladys, I suspect, had refused to leave her warm bed. In any case, there were no bombs, only the planes flying over Rickmansworth on their way to London. Never was I so relieved to hear the All Clear and to be allowed to go back to bed.

At school next morning we compared notes of the night's excitements. I found that nobody else had been made to kneel in a corner under a sack. People laughed when I told them, or thought I had made it up. It seemed that Mrs H was not a typical English housewife.

Things were getting worse and worse at the H's and we were feeling more and more unhappy. In desperation, I told Miss Ping how unhappy we were. We had been told to bring any complaints to our own headmistress. She listened very sympathetically and told us to try and put up with it a little longer; she would see what could be done about getting our billet changed. Some days later she said that it wasn't easy, that most people had their evacuees, but that she had spoken to a Mrs Baker from the WVS about us.

One day Lotte caught a bad cold. Mrs H did nothing about it and it got worse. She developed a very bad cough and though I mentioned this to Mrs H she took no notice, and told me not to fuss. Lotte seemed to me in very low spirits and feverish. I felt rather worried and so I took her round to Ruth's foster mother surreptitiously, asking her if she would be kind enough to take Lotte's temperature. She did have a temperature and I thought she ought to stay in bed, and not be made to go to school. Mrs G suggested that I take her to see a doctor and recommended a Dr Salmon.

'Why not go and see him now?'

I thought that if I told Mrs H she would only interfere and forbid me to take her and, as my vivid imagination had already painted Lotte languishing at death's door with double pneumonia, I decided simply to play truant from school and to take Lotte to Dr Salmon's surgery there and then.

This was quite an ordeal, because I did not know the procedure. I had never been to an English surgery before and whenever I had been to see the doctor, it had always been with Mummy. However, after waiting some time in the waiting-room, the doctor saw us and listened to my halting explanations. I think he seemed a little surprised to see two young children on their own. He asked me all sorts of questions about our circumstances and seemed very kind and understanding. Then he examined Lotte and said that indeed she should stop in bed. He prescribed some medicine and said that he would come and call in a few days.

This gave me courage to face Mrs H again. When I told her what the doctor had said, I didn't feel a bit afraid. She yelled at me and said that I had no business to go to doctors behind her back and what a secretive creature I was, to be sure. However, she had to allow Lotte to remain at home in bed; that was all that mattered.

Years later we heard Dr Salmon's version of our visit. Apparently he had been very impressed when two little skimpy refugee-evacuees arrived at his surgery demanding advice. He thought I had acted very responsibly and bravely, but had also been very amused.

Soon after this episode Mrs Baker, the chief billeting officer for the WVS, invited Lotte and me to tea at her own house. She was a marvellous person to be in charge of such a post. That visit marked the turning-point in our lives. Up till then I really had not known what to do, or where to turn. I had no idea what to do about our circumstances at the H's, all I did know was that we could not stay there much longer.

Entering Mrs Baker's house was like coming out of a prolonged blizzard into a warm and friendly room. She had silvery-grey hair and a young face with good bones and such kind blue eyes. She was not wearing her uniform. The house was an old one, beautifully furnished, with flowers about the place, pleasing pictures, comfortable chairs covered in warm colours and a thick pastel-shade carpet. A dainty trolley with pretty china teacups, cakes and thin slices of bread and butter and jam, was ready by her chair. She had taken trouble.

I think she must have noticed our pleased reaction when we

came into the room, where a bright fire was burning. She started chatting to us and soon got us talking and at our ease. She told us about her grown-up daughter and sons and that she had been to Germany many times, and how much she had enjoyed her holidays there. She got us talking about our parents and our interests, about music and finally about our problems at the H's.

It was difficult for us to tell her; it isn't nice to start complaining when one has been invited out to tea, but cleverly she elicited from us enough facts that made it pretty obvious to her that the billet was unsuitable, especially as the H's did not want to keep us anyway. Mrs Baker explained how hard it would be to find alternative accommodation, particularly as we wanted to stay together, but she really would try very hard and told us to come and see her again and to keep her informed of any new problems. At last I felt that we were not quite alone any more. It was a great help.

She said that she had enjoyed the afternoon too and had found it very interesting to talk to us. She seemed surprised at how good our English was. Then she showed us how to make buttonholes from beechnuts and acorns: they were painted up with bright enamel paints and the stalks had to be reinforced with special thread. She sold them at WVS functions for various war charities. We said we would collect nuts and she would give us the paint. It was good fun making them. Buttonholes were worn quite a lot in those days on coats and costumes, and people were patriotic and tended to buy them for a good cause. Near Christmas time she raised quite a bit of money with them.

12 Ports of Call

The weeks went by and sometimes Mrs Baker from the WVS would see us or send a message by Miss Ping to say that she hadn't forgotten us and was still trying hard to find us another billet. The H's were eager to be rid of us and threatened to put us out before Christmas. At last, one day towards the end of November, Mrs Baker summoned us and told us that she could promise nothing definite, and certainly nothing permanent, but would we go round the following afternoon after school to see a Mrs Salmon who lived in that big house on the Uxbridge Road, called Colne House. We were very excited.

It seemed an enormous house, standing well back from the road, behind a high wall. We had been told to go to the back door, so we opened a large wooden gate and went through a paved yard, up a flight of stone steps. From there we were able to see over a high fence which separated the yard from the garden. We gasped in wonder. We could see only part of it, but it seemed like a huge, ancient park with enormous old trees and sloping lawns.

Fearfully we pressed the bell and after a while a maid opened the door, wearing a black dress with white collar and cuffs and a gleaming white, starched apron, just a little one, with lace round the edges, and a small, starched cap on her head. We told her who we were.

'Madam is expecting you. Come along please.'

We stepped over the threshold into a large, bright kitchen, but were immediately called back and told to take off our wellingtons and to leave them outside the back door.

My heart sank. 'Oh dear,' I thought, 'they are fearfully strict and now we are already in disgrace.'

We followed the maid into the sitting-room, expecting the worst. We entered a high room with a large fireplace where a bright fire was leaping away, the flames dancing over the shiny brass fire-irons in the hearth. We were told to sit on two leather seats on either side of the fireplace.

Two ladies were sitting opposite us on a large, cushioned settee: one was elderly, wearing glasses, the other was much younger and slim, with dark hair drawn back from a pale, oval face, out of which very serious, but beautiful grey eyes looked at us intently. But both ladies smiled in a very heart-warming way as they welcomed us, and we began to feel less awed. They had nice voices too, warm and low, and they spoke slowly and clearly and in a much more agreeable way than Mrs H. They asked us our names, about our parents in an interested, kindly way. They enquired how we were getting on at school and why we did not want to stay with the H's. Then the elder of the two, who we now knew was Mrs Salmon, asked us if we would like to come and stay with them, and we just said with deep fervour, 'Oh yes!'

How lovely everything was here: the two french windows had heavy gold velvet curtains looped up at the side and the carpet glowed with a rich Persian pattern, and when the maid brought in the tea trolley with little sandwiches and pillowy scones with butter and home-made raspberry jam, I felt as though it was my birthday. There was also a sponge cake with cream and jam inside and icing sugar on top, like a sprinkling of snow; there were golden rock-buns with currants, and the cups and plates were delicate and pale green. Did they live like that every day I wondered?

Over tea Mrs Salmon explained that she had already two evacuees, also refugees from Germany, and there was unfortunately no question of our staying with them permanently, because it was too much work for Muriel, the maid. But we could come and spend Christmas with them at Colne House and stay on a bit afterwards, by which time she felt sure Mrs Baker would have found us another billet. I suppose they sensed our disappointment and the younger lady, Mrs Salmon's daughter,

Kathleen, asked us about Christmases in Germany and told us we should have a big Christmas tree. It was sad to think that this lovely place would only be yet another staging-post, but children live in the present and the prospect of leaving the H's and spending Christmas here blotted out the disappointment. We skipped off, hugging the news that we were to come with our things at the end of the following week.

Years later we heard the full story of Mrs Baker's struggles on our behalf. She had tried every possible place, but Rickmansworth was already bursting with evacuees, and the prospect of another couple – not just one – and German refugees at that, was too much for anyone to contemplate. Finally, when she had mentioned her difficulties to Mrs Salmon, the result was an impulsive offer to take us for a few weeks. Mrs Baker was as pleased as we were and I am glad to think we let her know how grateful we felt. It seems that the H's had really given her an ultimatum: they were going to have us out a week before Christmas at the latest.

And so it was that one Saturday morning we came with our cases and moved into Colne House.

Colne House had once been a coaching inn. It was on the main street, but all the rooms faced towards the garden except the 'lounge' – an enormous entrance hall that ran the whole length of the ground floor. It was very lofty and had a fireplace at one end.

'Stand in it and look up,' Mrs Salmon suggested, smiling. We did so and could see all the way up the big rectangular chimney to a patch of sky. At the other end of the lounge two Bechstein grand pianos stood facing each other, their black bulk easily accommodated in that huge room. Two pianos, though? We were told that Kathleen was a pianist and the two were for duets. The space between fireplace and pianos was bare of furniture, but the floor was covered with oriental rugs and along the blank wall on the street side were ranged chairs of heavy black wood with twisted legs, high backs and tapestry upholstery. By the fire were some grandfather chairs, some leather pouffes, and that, apart from two splendid lamps suspended from the ceiling, was all.

The whole house was well furnished and comfortable, but one room in particular always delighted me: that was the 'drawing-room', used only for special tea parties and evening gatherings, and more or less a closed Aladdin's cave to us. But sometimes I sneaked in and just looked. It was furnished with gilded chairs and inlaid tables and chests; there were silk cushions and lamp-shades and heavy blue velvet curtains with enormous pompoms at the end of thick cords, and lots of fragile porcelain figures. The floor was covered with a soft pinky carpet and the walls with silky striped material.

This room, like all the others, had french windows opening on to a long wooden veranda from which steps led down into the garden. In summer, Mrs Salmon told us, clusters of purple wisteria cascaded from the trellis-work. The bedrooms and bath-room were upstairs, also overlooking the garden. One wing of the house had been converted into a self-contained flat where Esther Hulbert, one of Kathleen's musical friends, lived with her widowed mother. Dr Salmon's consulting-rooms had been there before he retired.

And now for our domain! In the semi-basement there was another complete flat with its own back door. In more prosper-ous times it had been the servants' quarters. Now it was occupied only by Muriel, who combined the roles of cook, housekeeper, chambermaid and lady's maid with the help only of a part-time charwoman. Not far from Muriel's bed-sitting-room a bedroom had been prepared for Lotte and me. It was quite large, but the veranda projecting overhead made the room rather dark and unless one had the light on, it was always filled with shadows from which two brass bedsteads glinted in a friendly way. But there was one great advantage: if one climbed out of the window, one found oneself in a little dry moat that ran directly below the veranda, and from there one could creep out into the garden unobserved.

Next to our bedroom was a room that was henceforth called 'the playroom'. It had been an all-purpose room for cleaning shoes and silver and therefore had broad benches running right along the window side. It was much brighter too, because the veranda stopped at that point. It also contained the coke fuel boilers for the central heating of the whole house, so that it was warm, though occasionally rather smelly. It really made a lovely playroom: there was even a sink in the little pantry next door, so handy for painting!

Muriel used the big table for ironing. There always was an enormous pile after the week's washing and it took her two afternoons or evenings to get it all done. They were enjoyable evenings. There was a warm comfortable smell from the ironing;

the whole process was soothing and tranquil. Muriel used to starch her aprons and caps, tray-cloths, tablecloths and napkins and I liked to see the steam rise up and the linen emerge gleaming white, stiff and crackly. Muriel was usually in a good mood when ironing, and so we chatted to her and folded the handkerchiefs (120 one week) and hung up things on the clothes-horse. It was nice to be told, 'You *are* being a great help.' Apart from these occasional intrusions the playroom was our territory, except for Muriel's cats, Adam and Eve, who had their baskets beside the boiler during the winter.

Sometimes we still hardly dared to breathe in case the whole pack of cards collapsed. Since it had been impressed on us that our stay at Colne House was only temporary, I tried hard not to allow myself to become too involved or attached to anything. Although as the days passed and nothing was said, I sometimes dreamed that perhaps we might be allowed to stay.

I had my fourteenth birthday at Colne House and a visit from Tante Rosel and my cousin who brought my parents' birthday letters, which had been posted nearly a month before, so that I should be sure of having their good wishes on time.

Those letters suddenly revived my longing for my parents most poignantly. So many things had been happening to us lately and so fast, that temporarily I did not have time to fret.

For my birthday my father wrote:

My beloved Child,
For the first time we are far away from you on your birthday – we cannot take you into our arms, we cannot give you kisses, we cannot prepare your birthday-table with gifts, but what we still *can* do, thank God, is to think of you with deepest love and pray and hope with all our heart for your happiness and well-being; let that be a comfort and joy to you on your fourteenth birthday. And we know that your thoughts also are with us and so we are together in spirit at least.

Now it is Lotte, our *Nesthäckchen* who is the representative of the whole family (since Inge won't have time to see you during the week). Well, Lotte has seen often enough at home how one manages such occasions, and I am sure she'll do it well, even if there won't be chicken and rice!

It is almost like a symbol that you should be far from home for the first time on your fourteenth birthday, since that marks the transition from childhood into adolescence, the beginning of taking responsibility for oneself! How I should have liked to ease just that particular step for you, but we put our confidence in you that you will find your own way . . .

Both your and Lotte's birthday presents will have to stand credited to you. In the meantime, on this important day, accept your father's blessing, that blessing that I send to you every Friday evening in thought. You remember the *Fervorechecho*, the prayer on which Mummy's tongue always got twisted!

'May the Lord bless you and keep you; may the Lord make his face to shine on you and give you his peace!' And this goes for Lotte too. And now look up, and may your new year bring us together again *soon* and preserve you from pain, of which you have had a great deal this past year through the death of your dear Uncle Ala. And one *urgent* request: please, please do write to us once a week, a letter or a card with a little greeting from Lotte too . . .

When that was written my parents had not heard that we were with the Salmons, but by 17 December the news had caught up with them. My mother wrote:

My darling children,
    That was a great and joyful occasion for us this morning when the postman brought your two postcards – the first news from you in *seven* weeks! I find it so hard to bear to be without news from you for so long and get very anxious. Other acquaintances have letters from their children every week. *Please* don't leave us without news for quite so long again.
    And now you are living with such a kind doctor's family who even allowed you to invite children for your birthday! I was surprised to hear that you had changed your address, but Egon writes that you have such a kind young foster mother who gives you Spanish lessons, dear Hannele, and that you are very well looked after. There must have been some reason though for your change of accommodation – were you not well cared for before? We are very relieved that you are now in such good hands. And so the house is 'almost like a castle'! . . .
    You can imagine how glad we are that you are with such a kind family and with a doctor at that, who will keep an eye on

your health. You well know what *that* means to me! I hope you are keeping your things tidy and not making too much unnecessary work. I too am glad that you are no longer having to sleep in one bed.

That you get such good marks at school, dear Lotte, pleases us very much. What about you, Hannele dear? And now it seems that you are in need of a brassière! Can't you send us a photograph? Liesel Heilbronner sent one to her parents – she too has grown. Try and let us know how tall both of you are now and how much you weigh.

Do you still have your little threepenny bottom, dear Lotte? How I long to give it a little pinch. Do you really wash yourself all by yourself now, and thoroughly too? What time does school start with you? And you are reading such interesting books, dear Hannele, quite like your Daddy. Last week Marlies Berg and her parents left for Belgium [where Marlies and her mother survived in hiding until the end of the war]. As usual, Daddy accompanied them on the train for part of the way . . . There are not many of our acquaintances left now . . .

Apart from everything else, this letter gave us hope of Daddy's and Mummy's chances of getting out of Germany soon, in spite of the war. Had not the Bergs escaped to Belgium?

Christmas was coming and presents had to be made for everybody. In those days, decorated blotters, hand-painted calendars, egg cosies, raffia mats and baskets, beaded pin-cushions and the inevitable buttonholes were our stock-in-trade. The Christmas tree arrived and was erected in the lounge by Mr Bourne, the gardener, and the four of us, Betty, Charlotte, Lotte and I, with Kathleen supervising, were allowed to decorate the tree. It was very tall, reaching from the ground nearly to the high ceiling and when we had finished it looked very beautiful with its coloured glass balls and baubles, although I missed the real candles of our tree at home.

Kathleen, who was a fervent Catholic convert, had taken a large and poor Catholic family under her wing and felt that such a lovely tree ought to be enjoyed by as many children as possible. So on Christmas afternoon a crowd of children came to a Christmas party with cake, hats, balloons and party games. But before that we had our first splendid English Christmas dinner with roast turkey and Christmas pudding with little silver trinkets hidden inside it, each carefully wrapped in greaseproof paper. There was a little silver 'bachelor's button', an 'old maid's thimble', a boot, a ship and other delightful objects. It was such an exciting custom and Lotte and I took every mouthful with great caution, while Auntie (as Mrs Salmon wanted to be called) watched us with a mischievous, knowing look, probably having contrived that we should find something in our helpings. That first year it was a boot I found, which had to be returned later, to be used again the following year, but in exchange we received silver threepenny bits.

I remember feeling very happy at the end of the day and asking anxiously if we had to leave Colne House now that Christmas was over, but Kathleen assured me that we should be staying a while yet. The Christmas days passed and no one referred to the end of our stay; we did not mention it either, in case, by speaking of it, we made it happen. Like ostriches we buried our fears, although deep down the uncertainty remained.

New Year's Eve had come and there was to be a big party for the grown-ups – preparations had been going on all day. Kathleen called me to her and to my unspeakable surprise and delight she said, 'You're a big girl now, fourteen, and I think that you are old enough to stay up to see the New Year in.'

I felt speechless and very proud to be thus singled out. Betty was away with relatives over the holidays; Lotte and Charlotte had to go to bed and I tried to dress myself as smartly as I could. It was a very civilized affair and I felt really happy to be part of them all and included in their conversations. The food was delicious and everyone was sweet to me. Midnight came, the bells were ringing and everybody kissed everybody else. We wished each other a happy New Year and everybody expressed the hope that it would bring me a reunion with my parents. Then we all joined hands, making a big circle and sang something which I now know to be 'Auld Lang Syne', but at the time it seemed a strange and moving custom.

We later heard how my parents had spent their first New Year's Eve of separation. This letter reached us much later, but it was very moving. My father treats my fervent declarations very gently and an undertone of serious counsel gives the letter an almost valedictory tone.

My dearest children,

Today I will answer your letter of 15 December 1939 by typewriter, so that you can read everything I have to say. First of all I must tell you that we were 'terribly' pleased with your letters, particularly as they came before the end of the old year. That raised our spirits on New Year's Eve and at midnight we drank your health in a glass of punch.

From all sides we hear that you are both well; that you, dear Hannele, have grown and developed and that your new foster parents are looking after you so admirably. This in particular makes us feel happy and reassured, and we beg you to tell them *how grateful* we feel for all they are doing for you.

I can well believe you, dear Lotte, that you enjoy Hannele reading to you from our classics – Hauff, Uhland, Schiller – but I hope you are also reading books in your new language. I too read to your mother and grandparents (who are back with us now, indefinitely, since they can no longer live in Pirmasens), but usually amusing stories, so that they don't fall asleep . . . And now I am coming to your warm and loving letter, my Hannekin. Yes, thank God, you *are* still a child, even though you are now a *Backfisch.* You need not be afraid that your 'lovely youth is over' and you need not long for its return. Keep your faith in God. Your childhood may perhaps be over as far as actual years are concerned, but you are only standing at the start of your youth and you have – as I am told from all sides – dear and kind people who are being father and mother to you and bringing you up in our stead. Inge and Egon visit you often and I am only sorry that Tante Rosel can't look in on you because of her bad leg.

Yes of course, dear Hannele, I do know *what* you mean and I do understand. It is only natural that you are homesick for us, for you have had in our lovely home, through your good teachers and your occasionally strict, but all too often indulgent parents, a *truly happy* childhood. Remember it in your heart for the rest of your life; it can be a comfort later on in many a hardship, which everyone has to experience in the course of life.

I am glad you recognize how all the good things you have had (and still have, thank God) are not there as a matter of course, but have to be deserved through love, obedience and gratitude. There is no harm in blaming yourself for some of the things you have done in the past, or in now making firm resolutions for the future. But you do know that it's easy to *make* resolutions, to *carry them out* is more difficult. All the more satisfying then, when you do carry them out, to know that you give pleasure to others, particularly to your parents, who are always with you in thought. The older you get, the more you will find that there is more satisfaction in giving than in receiving.

But both of you are still so young that you may unhesitatingly give yourselves up to any good and decent pleasures joyfully, without restraint. Do believe, dear child, we shall soon be together again, wherever it may be, and there will be many opportunities yet for you to experience our love for you, and for proving your love for us.

It's clear that God means well towards you, because first he sent you to Tante Rosel and Onkel Ala . . . and now, once again, you have found a home with such good people. So you must not be ungrateful to your fate, even though you are quite right when you say that our separation is a test – a test that we want to pass, don't we?

You do remember what I have always told you? Shun and hate lying – it is the root of all evil. Rather take upon you any punishment, than through lying, escape punishment. And lastly, try to become (or continue to be) obedient; don't make people have to tell you three or four times what only has to be done in the end anyway.

I was very touched by your remark that you want to make yourself and Lotte into 'good, honest people'. I hope that you are honest already, but thank God, you have always been honest children and will remain so, I am sure. When one has such good intentions, you'll just have to bear them in mind, and I am sure you will be good.

And so you have already reached the age of 'crushes'! What a big daughter I have. I used to adore girls secretly too at your age, but I would have felt *terribly* embarrassed if they had had any inkling of this. I hope that you too will act according to this recipe.

Now you have had enough of fatherly advice. Just stay well and we will too and *please, please*, write to us every two weeks, and one letter to Tante Rosel every two weeks – that means only *one* letter every Sunday . . . We are now waiting again longingly for your next letter . . .

Early in the new year the snow came and the large lawn rolled away from the house, a thick, inflated eiderdown, blue-white and glittering, down towards the black water of the Colne. Only the black scribbles of the twigs and branches by the river-bank and the dark thicket of the spinney, where owls hooted at night, scored the perfect whiteness. The snow erased all imperfections and sadness, and a sort of holiday feeling took possession of me. I loved coming into the warmth from the white wastes and the snowball-fights and outdoor activities, tired and glowing, content and looking forward to tea and cosiness.

13 Haven

But the first week of the new year was not yet over when Auntie told us that we were going to be 'boarded out', as Kathleen wasn't well enough to go on looking after us all at present. A temporary billet had been found for Lotte and me and another one for Betty, while Charlotte, who was the youngest and whose parents were in London and about to take her to America, was allowed to remain.

This came as a real shock. Up welled that sense of uncertainty – was this just an excuse to be rid of us?

'Are we really coming back?' I asked anxiously.

'Yes, quite definitely, after two weeks,' was the answer. 'You can leave most of your things here and come and visit us for tea on Saturday.' So that was an insurance, and knowing that it was to be only a temporary absence made it easier to put up with yet another change. But we still couldn't start settling down or relaxing; the prospect seemed one of changes and readjustment.

I recently found an old diary for 1940 in which our temporary banishment from Colne House is recorded in the double cipher of German and the obscure Gothic script we had been taught at primary school. On the cover is written in clear English print: 'To be burnt unread in case of my death.'

[Friday, 5 January I wrote:] Today was an important day. We had to leave our kind Salmons for two weeks; thank God, only for two weeks! I wish they were over already. We felt anxious the whole day, wondering where we were going and what it would be like.

[Monday, 8 January:] For breakfast we had toast, soaked deep in fat and two little greasy sausages. I felt quite sick and didn't know how to force them down, particularly the toast. Luckily the lady left the room and I deftly swiped the sausages into my knickers – they felt hot and slippery. The fried toast I slipped into the front of my satchel. I had to laugh when I looked across at Lotte, who sat there open-mouthed . . .

Mr Rowlands is back. I'm so glad because I've got a real crush on him. He really is sweet with his black hair and crooked smile. He is very clever. I am very proud to be a *Backfisch* now. I shall try to behave as they do in books. Yesterday Ruth came back from her holidays with an aunt in Northwood. I am glad, because now I have someone to talk to about Mummy and Daddy. I think we are well suited for friends, since we have similar fates. I hope there won't be any greasy sausages tomorrow!

[Tuesday, 9 January:] Today it was very nice in school. We've done a lot of work. In February we are going to have exams – I'll have to do a lot of swotting and catching up. Mr Rowlands gave me twenty logarithms to do. I went through torture trying to do them. Rowlands is very sweet and decent, giving me *twenty* sums! I'll behave in his class and pay attention. He was wearing a new dark suit today and looked fit to eat. Only another ten days, then back to the Salmons!

[Wednesday, 10 January:] This morning, oh horror! Greasy sausages! And she didn't leave the room. Quite nice in school. Cirrul [sic] Rowlands was pleased with me because I got all my sums right. I'm getting on well with Ruth and we have fun, particularly about Cirrul – he is such a stunner and walks like a dancer and he is so clever. We are writing a poem about him.

[Thursday, 11 January:] I've *had* to tell her! Very politely I said that she need not give us sausages every morning and that we didn't need fried toast either.

[Friday, 12 January:] I don't mind Rowlands teasing me in a

good-natured way, even about my accent, but I do object to being treated like a performing monkey. He knows I can't pronounce my 'rs' and today he made me say 'trigonometry' in front of the whole class. Of course I said 'tchigenometchy'.

'Again!' he yells and 'Again!'

I go redder and redder and more and more embarrassed and the tears come to my eyes. He really can be cruel, trying to make me a laughing-stock in front of the whole class. I hate him. But I think the children were on my side though.

[Saturday, 13 January:] Today we had *six* sausages – three at breakfast and three at midday. Luckily she was out at midday. I ate one and wrapped the other two in my handkerchief and hid them in my pants. Later I pushed one into a waterpipe out of doors and I buried the other. I do feel homesick for Mummy and Daddy.

[Wednesday, 17 January:] Only another two days! The food situation is getting worse and worse here. I'm starving! In the mornings we get porridge now (no more sausages!) but it's always burnt. In the afternoons we have bread and butter and tea, but they have eggs and cakes in front of us, even the baby! In the evening it's just a cup of cocoa. I feel quite miserable. Today I was told to go to bed at a quarter to eight – and I a *Backfisch*! I felt so humiliated. I have no intention of going *so* early. Haven't heard from Tante Rosel and feel a bit worried, because of her leg, and awfully alone. I keep longing for Mummy and Daddy and I can't help thinking and brooding about them at night. What *is* going to happen? I hate all this uncertainty.

[Friday, 19 January:] What a disappointment! Today after school we were supposed to go back to the Salmons, but at break Mr Wightman (the headmaster) called me into his office and gave me a letter from Kathleen. It was a kind letter but it carried bad news.

'Dear Penny and Twopence,

I am not quite well enough yet to look after you and so we have found somewhere else for you to go, just for one more week. I really hope it won't have to be any longer. Come to tea tomorrow.'

I felt bitterly disappointed and Lotte too, when I told her the news during playtime. I do feel miserable – it's so hard to get used to different strangers almost *every* week. This is the fourth foster home since leaving Hampstead.

These new people are quite nice – they seem a lot cleaner. They have got gaslight. But they seem very nosy and it's a bit embarrassing because they canoodle in front of us. I wonder what this first night here will be like?

[Friday, 26 January:] Back to the Salmons this afternoon. We were welcomed back very warmly and with genuine pleasure. Nice feeling. We shall have to be very good and obedient and help Muriel a lot, so that we don't get sent away again. Betty has gone for good. They found her another billet.

I shall not go to the cinema any more on Saturday mornings, but save my money for a shorthand/typing course. We had another letter from Mummy and Daddy. Charlotte's father, Dr Alexander, who was staying at Colne House, asked if he could read it. He was very nice and said, 'That's a wonderfully written letter.' I felt very proud. I'll try awfully hard to become a good person. Today we had fish and chips at school, my favourite food.

[Thursday, 1 February:] Today Mr R was examined for the air force; he is joining up. Pity. Outside it's terribly squelchy. Kathleen is getting a bit mean with the bathwater – I was allowed only two inches. [I suspect Kathleen was following official advice that baths should be limited to four inches of water.] Had a quarrel with Lotte today; I really must try not to quarrel with her – after all, I am supposed to be in Mother's stead, though sometimes she can be infuriating.

[Saturday, 3 February:] Lovely day! It seems Auntie wanted to be rid of us today, so she gave us some money for Saturday morning cinema – *Queen of the Jungle*. It was fantastic. I'd love to go again every Saturday, but I must save. Lovely lunch. I love my food here now very much. Kathleen gave us a *compotition* [This word, thus spelt, was in English] today. I got 110 words right and am going to get a little prize. She takes her task of 'bringing us up' very seriously, sometimes it gets a bit much, but we shall have to play along with her, because Auntie says it gives her a real responsibility and something important to occupy her mind after her unhappy love affair in Spain. We are her war-work.

[Tuesday, 13 February:] Charlotte Alexander is leaving Rickmansworth next week; she is going back to London to her parents and then all of them are going to America. Pity, because then Lotte will be without a friend of her own age – they got on so well together. Ruth too is taking an exam for a child-nursery. Her uncle will have to pay for it, but it means that I too shall be left without my confidante. Ruth will at least have some sort of training, but I shan't be able to become a foreign corre-spondent . . .

Sometimes I imagine that we might get a letter tomorrow from Mummy and Daddy saying, 'We are safely in America, come and join us!' Perhaps it will happen *one* day; if only they stay well.

[Friday, 6 February:] A fateful day! It began well and ended in disaster. Charlotte and I had little colds. To be honest, mine was mainly pretence, because I was wanting a day off from school for a change, a day with particularly difficult sums. But I learnt to regret my truancy.

Well, we were treated like little princesses and got our meals in bed and everybody was sweet to us and spoilt us. We were given drinks. I loved this sort of indulgence and Charlotte and I had great fun together till – well, till it happened.

Kathleen came down bringing me her own smart camel-hair coat, saying that when I have to go to the lavatory across the cold stone passage I was to be sure to wear it. 'And don't get out of bed except to go to the toilet.'

I had every intention of taking great care and of doing as she told me. Then I remembered that my fountain-pen needed fill-ing, so that I could write my diary. But the ink was in the playroom. So I obediently put on the coat and went to fetch the ink. The ink-bottle wasn't properly shut. I returned to my room and went to the chest to fill my pen, when suddenly I became aware of something flowing over my feet. I looked down and – the beautiful coat of which I was to take particular care, stared at me blue with ink. I was in despair. I think I must have pulled out half my hair, tugging at it in desparation. I didn't know *what* to do and kept calling on God and on Charlotte to help me. She sat there open-mouthed and speechless, just goggling, which didn't help. For a brief moment I considered suicide. Then I started scrubbing and rubbing away at it, keeping up a lamentation, 'Oh dear, I *know* I'm going to be sent away for ever!' I remembered Mummy once calling me 'Hans Huckebein, *der Unglücksrabe*' (a story about someone who was forever in trouble, just as I was). I took the coat to the pantry and continued rubbing with water, and indeed it seemed to me that the blue was growing paler. But as I returned to the room a terrible sight met my eyes! I almost collapsed with horror, because the carpet displayed a sizeable blue lake. I quickly got all the blotting-paper I could find and fetched Lotte's tooth-salt and covered the large blot, then took no more notice of the carpet, as the coat seemed to me of primary importance.

And now I was sitting in bed, thinking hard how best to break it to Kathleen. I kept getting out of bed and looking at the coat every minute, to decide if the stains had improved; if, in fact, one might not even notice them. At last I came to the decision to be quite honest about it. I seemed to hear Daddy say: 'Be honest and take your punishment.' Actually there wasn't anything else I could do.

It seemed that God had mercy, because when K came down with our dinner (my appetite had quite disappeared), I had an idea. I thought that if I could really cry it might arouse her softer feelings. I felt so miserable so it wasn't hard to cry. No sooner was she through the door, than I called to her weeping, 'Are you very cross with me, and will you send me away now? It wasn't *really* my fault, the bottle wasn't shut; I tried to make it better, but . . . I'm so *sorry.*'

She didn't know *what* I was talking about. I must have presented the most wretched face, for suddenly she began to laugh. That gave me a little more courage and I began to explain the situation to her. I'm afraid her laughter vanished quite, when she saw her coat. But all she said was, 'Dry your tears and eat your dinner; I'll try and clean the coat.'

I asked her again whether I should now be sent away, but she said, 'No, you needn't be afraid of that.'

I was already so glad that it had all ended so well, when her eyes fell on the stained carpet! That was too much. Then she started telling me off and I felt that I quite deserved it.

'This is always what happens when you are disobedient. I told you not to leave your bed. Well, it can't be helped, but promise me in future to do as you are told; I don't tell you these things for nothing.'

I felt she was quite right. In fact I thought her very tolerant. Then it was all over. Something to tell my grandchildren, I thought, relieved.

[Thursday, 7 March:] I haven't heard from Mummy and Daddy for such a long time now and am very worried. What can have happened? Please dear God, make it all come right in the end. In school we got a new teacher who takes us for history, English and geography. He is brilliant. He reminds me a little of Daddy in the days when he was still young and beautiful. He explains everything so clearly and goes quite deeply into everything and discusses it with us, like Daddy used to do. It's the first time that I have actually remembered anything taught in history. Unfortunately he is here only for one week. Yesterday I stayed in school till six, doing extra work.

[Sunday, 10 March:] Saturday. A beautiful day today. In the morning we helped Muriel and did our chores, then we mooched about the kitchen until Muriel threw us out. Then we took our weekly way down to town to Woolworths and Boots, then we looked in all the shop-windows. When we got home Muriel told us that Charlotte was coming down with her mother to say goodbye. We collected them from the station. Kathleen later took photographs of us all and Mrs Alexander was very sweet to us and gave Lotte and me *three* shillings! On the 15th they are finally leaving for America. I wished them happiness and thought deep down – if only we too could be reunited with our parents soon.

[Wednesday, 13 March:] A heavenly day! At breakfast this morning there lay beside our plate, quite unexpectedly, the most wonderful present – a letter from M & D. My whole day at school and everywhere was brightened by it; I felt as light as air. They wrote so lovingly and my longings for them are made more intense by seeing their writing and reading their words. Soon it is Passover and soon it is darling Mummy's birthday. But something they mentioned in the letter which filled me with gloom: namely that we have to be patient, as it seems that it will be a long time yet before we can be reunited. Something to do with documents, dollars and such things. But I have to try and be strong, as M & D have begged us to be in the letters, and to go on trusting in God. I will try.

And so the entries continue for a few more weeks, mingling the daily routine of school, scrapes and little treats, good resolutions, especially to study hard, with childish adolescence: 'We have deep snow; I'm missing my toboggan very much. I am wearing my German track-suit all the time in this weather, and though I say it myself, I like myself in it. Hope Mr Rowlands catches a glimpse of me in it.'

And of course, always as a continuous undertow runs the anxiety about my parents and longing for them to come to England.

Meanwhile, in America, Uncle Max and Walter (another Walter, my father's cousin) were trying hard to provide the guarantees that would enable them to go to the United States. But communication was very slow.

It has depressed us considerably to learn that we can't take the children with us to America. As far as our own affairs are concerned . . . we need about twenty documents from Walter and others, [wrote my mother] on top of that comes the all-important question of dollars for our passage. We have not yet heard from Walter or Max. Even if everything goes according to plan, it'll be summer by the time we can go. For the children it might perhaps be better if they joined us later, but that is an idea I find hard to accept . . .

[And a little later my mother wrote:] No, my dear Hannele, we have not yet been to Stuttgart [the American Consulate]. First we need papers from the States and the dollars for our passage, and only when *all* the papers are in order shall we be notified from Stuttgart to attend. But it takes a *terribly* long time for letters to reach us from America . . .

[And yet again:] You are wrong, Hannele, if you think we are delaying in order to bring a lot of things with us – only the absolute necessities, and possibly not even those. It really is not our fault if we are not yet ready to emigrate. That is simply and entirely due to the long delays of letters coming from America – they seem to take about three months.

When additional guarantees were required, Daddy wrote to inform cousin Walter, and now we are waiting for the answer . . . You know we are longing to be reunited with you two *Hascherl*. It disappointed us very much to find that we cannot all go to America together, but since we cannot alter it, we shall have to accept it.

Herr Schnook, your old teacher, asked after you. I don't know how many pupils are left in your class now – not many. [Herr Schnook, a pale young teacher with a quiet voice was a man of great courage and conviction. Although teachers and children left daily in a steady stream to escape to safety, Herr Schnook did not even try to emigrate. He felt it to be his duty to stand by those last few unfortunate children who remained. Both he and his wife were finally deported.]

Our American business is progressing *very* slowly. Sometimes Daddy explodes. You know the picture.

The transformation in my mother revealed in these and other letters never ceases to astonish me. Her calm courage and stoic acceptance of the inevitable were not characteristics that had been very evident in her earlier, rather protected life. Now she was practical and clear-sighted and a great support to my father.

For some time after our temporary absence from Colne House I felt very insecure, as if I was on probation; I felt that I was allowed to stay *only* if I were a 'good girl': obedient, helpful and careful. It seems that Lotte, three-and-a-half years younger, never felt this. It may have been that in spite of my good intentions, I wasn't the tidiest or most practical of people and did get into trouble.

Muriel quite justifiably complained of the extra work we made, because much of it fell on her and, as Auntie told us later, it took some persuading to get her to accept our staying on. Like us, she had been under the impression that it was to have been a temporary stay, but gradually it became implicitly accepted that we were to stay for the duration of the war, or until we were able to join our parents, when they got out of Germany.

Muriel's feelings were understandable. She too had been a

protégée of Auntie's when she first came to England from the Wales of the depression. Auntie had been her first employer and by now they had been together for about ten years. But in spite of our mutual frictions and jealousies, we became quite fond of each other and I found her companionable and motherly. I loved her methodical ways and her sense of order. I suppose I found it reassuring in an unstable world, particularly as I lacked these qualities in myself. Everything was done regularly and thoroughly and to time. Originally there had been several servants in the house, but the war and Uncle's (Dr Salmon's) retirement had put a stop to that.

Monday was washday, when we had bubble-and-squeak and cold meat with chutney and beetroot – a meal I adored. All morning Muriel would be toiling in the wash-house, a small stone building attached to the old servants' quarters, where a huge zinc copper pan was steaming and bubbling, whites were being stirred in blue bags and starch and I would occasionally help to turn the mangle. By lunchtime Muriel always reckoned to have cleaned up and to have the washing blowing on the line.

Every day after lunch was cleared away Muriel was supposed to be free till teatime. She would wash herself from top to toe with beautifully scented soap. Then she would change her morning dress of pale blue or green cotton for her afternoon outfit of back dress, white collar, cuffs and dainty lace-edged apron with cap to match. Auntie used to give her these outfits for Christmas together with some new material for making herself morning dresses.

In Muriel's room there stood rows of good leather shoes. She was very fond of good shoes and took great care of them, perhaps because she had sometimes gone barefoot in Wales. On a certain day of the week she would polish all her shoes till they looked like new. The rest of the afternoons she would sit by her fire, either writing letters or knitting. She was a most skilful and rapid knitter and all her cardigans and jumpers were hand-made in matching shades of greens, browns and ochres. When she got her weekly magazines, the *Church Weekly* and a woman's magazine, she would sit quietly reading everything. Sometimes, during the holidays or weekends, she would bring her knitting into the playroom. On special occasions she allowed us to come into her room and chat with her, but we were only allowed to go there by invitation. I didn't really like her room. Like all the basement rooms, it was rather dark, but hers never seemed to get the sun at all.

Later, when she had perforce accepted us, I think Muriel quite enjoyed coming to sit with us, chatting, while we drew or played; sometimes she even vented mild complaints about 'Madam' or 'Miss Kathleen'. She would join in games with us and occasionally we might invite her to a little 'tea-party', calling her 'Mrs Jones', which became a pet-name for her.

Muriel, like most Welsh people, was very musical and had a lovely clear singing voice. She joined local choirs and they were her main outside interest. On her half-days she would visit her cousin Eva in Watford, or her sister Gwynneth, who was also 'in service'; a busy, if not very exciting life, but she agreed with Auntie that though the pay was little, she had a good home.

She was a wonderful cook of good English food. Food, in those days, was very important to me – as my diaries bear witness. Muriel prided herself on having a 'cool pastry hand', and with particular joy I remember her apple, gooseberry and blackcurrant pies, served with custard at Sunday dinners. Her teatime scones were delicious too, fluffy and warm with a dusting of flour and a hint of cream of tartar.

Altogether, 'English Tea' was a lovely institution, I thought, particularly at the weekends when we were at home for family tea at four o'clock. It was served in the sitting-room on a trolley with embroidered tray-cloths. Everybody would drift in from all the corners of the house and garden. For us children there always was a plate of thin slices of bread and butter. They had to be eaten first. Then there might be freshly baked scones with butter and raspberry jam, and when visitors were present there would probably be delicate cucumber sandwiches and a fragrant sponge cake, made that very day.

But the garden was the most marvellous thing that could have happened to me just then. I had never had a real garden in the English sense and would never have dreamt of one like this. A vast lawn rolled from the veranda steps down to the little river Colne, where the grass was allowed to grow long and soft, and all sorts of wild flowers bloomed between. Several old trees grew on the bank, their knobbly roots reaching right down into the water. Three large willow trees trailed their feathery skirts in the water. A maternal horse-chestnut provided us with all the conkers we wanted. I was especially fond of a large copper beech, because if

I climbed as far as the first fork, I would be completely hidden from the house by the thick, burnished foliage. There, or in a nest of long grass, I sometimes used to hide on summer afternoons, escaping with Baroness Orczy, or Rider Haggard, or Jeffrey Farnol, sometimes even deaf to the voices calling from the house. At other times I simply mooned about, gazing at the clouds and water. I found such things very comforting. Occasionally swans trailed past and ducks, and in the reeds an old rowing-boat lay rotting. It belonged to a period when Kathleen and Harold, her brother, were younger and friends had come for house parties and weekends. Later the boat was patched up and Lotte and I were allowed to use it.

On one side of the lawn lay the spinney, a dark, creepy copse, where trees and bushes grew very close together, covered in ivy and the sun never penetrated to the ground. On the other side, and separated by a splendid flowerbed and a hedge, were the orchard and kitchen gardens. I had never seen such abundance! Everything was there from apples and pears and plums to peaches and soft fruits. All this was very important in wartime. I remember how each summer and autumn we helped Muriel and Auntie to prepare beans for salting down and fruit for bottling – so much topping and tailing! It was always a thrill to watch Muriel test the Kilner jars the next morning to see how many had sealed and could safely join the colourful rows of preserves and jams in the storeroom.

Our joy in this abundance was a little diminished by the absolute prohibition to pick any fruit; everything was needed for preserving 'in these days of shortages'. During the height of summer we were allowed to eat as many windfall apples as we wanted, and Auntie had no use for the mulberries, that were simply left to drop, making purple splashes all around in the green grass. There we gorged, enjoying the subtle flavour of those translucent drupes that is so impossible to describe, but so unforgettable, that I can still taste it, although I have not eaten any mulberries since.

All this, and the greenhouse for indoor plants, was presided over by Mr Bourne, the gardener. I don't know how he managed it all. When we first came he had a boy to help him, but soon all the gardeners' boys were called up. That left Mr Bourne, a spare old man with a narrow face and soft baby skin – not at all hardened or weather-beaten – and rosy cheeks. He had young blue eyes and silvery wisps of hair and an even wispier moustache, rather like the quivering whiskers of a cat. He always wore the same old tweed jacket and a dark blue apron with a big pocket in front. He was quite old then and worked on until he died. Although he got slower and slower, somehow the garden got dug, the seeds sown, the roses and fruit trees pruned, the flowerbeds and greenhouse tended and the big lawn mown with a large motor-mower.

Occasionally Kathleen sallied forth to dig dandelions out of the lawn. She would show us how it was done and then hand over the tool. We all had to do our bit.

Mr Bourne's tool shed was near the old mulberry tree, where he ate his sandwiches for lunch. In the early days of our stay at Colne House, when the other two evacuees were still there, he used to regard us children just as another nuisance, like mice and sparrows. Gradually he came to accept us as inevitable and even talked to us about the garden and the weather. He had gaps in his teeth and spoke in a whistly sort of way. I could never understand how he coped with all this heavy work -- he looked like a bright autumn leaf about to be blown away.

14 Problems and a Solution

Now that I was fourteen I was due to leave school at the end of term, but I certainly did not feel equipped to earn a living. For one thing my English, though improving fast, was still imperfect and, of course, I had no formal qualifications. My father's letters dwelt on the subject. He was only too aware that he could no longer plan our lives, but he still did all he could by way of advice and encouragement. He was very anxious that I should not leave school:

> But you, Hannele, should on no account leave school yet. Talk to your headmaster and see if it is not possible for you to repeat the 8th class. Which school is your friend Ruth transferring to? Is there no chance that you could go there too? If there is a technical, or business, or domestic science school in your neighbourhood that would be the most useful thing. But if not, then simply sit through your last year again and pay particular attention to the subjects in which you are weakest. Perhaps you will have more sympathetic teachers in physics and history the second time round – you might even find yourself having a 'crush' on one of them!

He suggested that I should look into the possibility of an apprenticeship with a fashion house, for he knew I was interested in clothes and always making 'fashion drawings'. And he assured me that I need not despair of ever becoming a foreign correspondent: if I learnt shorthand and typing I could start as a secretary and work my way up, going to evening classes as he had done.

Perhaps you really have a natural bent and it will not be for nothing that you were born on Marlitt's hundredth birthday. In any case, it will do no harm if you try now and then to write down little experiences . . . But why, dear Hannele, do you sound so full of anxiety on our behalf? You may be certain that we – just as much as you – want to be reunited with you and we are doing *everything* that is necessary. But we cannot force things . . . But *three* months ago I wrote to Walter and Max by airmail and to this day I don't know if my letter ever got there . . . Next time you write could you enclose a nice letter for your old teacher, Herr Schnook, and for your class.

Today I saw some children in the tram who were reading *Nesthäckchen* – then I started feeling very homesick for you again. Just you wait, my darling bookworm, if I catch you out reading too much trash – I'll give you a cuff!

And now my darlings, keep well, greet your doctor's family heartily, be kissed and cuddled and nose-rubbed by your

Papi

I certainly didn't want to leave school yet, and Kathleen and Auntie thought it would be a pity, especially as I had no School Certificate. But the only secondary schools in Rickmansworth were a Convent School, St Joan of Arc's High School for Girls or the Royal Masonic school. The latter had received Aylwin, a London grammar school, as part of the evacuation scheme. Lotte was young enough to sit the Eleven Plus scholarship exam and perhaps transfer to the Aylwin. I was too old for that; so for me it was St Joan's or nothing. And where was the money to come from? The Salmons could not be expected to find it. Indeed, Auntie felt that the government allowance for evacuees did not cover the standard of living we were enjoying, which was certainly true. Tante Rosel paid some extra money occasionally and sent us our pocket-money, though she could ill-afford it.

Then one day I was told by Kathleen to tidy myself and to come upstairs to meet a Miss Lucy Stern, who might be able to help with my schooling. I was told that she too was Jewish and a teacher of English at Stroud in Gloucestershire. Very timidly I went upstairs and was introduced to a lady with short dark hair, rosy cheeks and a grave expression that at first struck me as rather severe. But when I looked at her eyes, I saw that she was really not so frightening at all. They were light brown with little gold flecks in them, bright and alert and quite humorous.

She was very pleasant to me and asked me questions about school and what I wanted to do, and why I wanted to stay on. She asked me about my parents and all sorts of things, so that I quite forgot what she had come for. She was pleased that I liked writing compositions and reading poetry and that I wrote little poems myself.

Then she told me that she wanted to do something to help people in the war, and she would rather help an individual person, than simply give a donation to some fund or other. Perhaps she could help with my schooling? It all seemed 'too good to be true'. Daddy was right: one did have to trust in life and things did always work out. I felt deeply grateful to Miss Stern and to Kathleen and Auntie too for trying so hard to find someone to help. As soon as everything was settled I wrote to Tante Rosel, and Egon composed a Red Cross letter to my parents. Six months later, in December, we had a reply: a short Red Cross message in which they acknowledged the news gratefully. Miss Stern had succeeded in bringing comfort to two desperately tried and worried individuals.

Later I learnt of the extraordinary set of coincidences that had led to the appearance of Miss Stern as my benefactress. She told me that she had been at home in Heronsgate during her school holidays, feeling very worried and upset by the Nazi atrocities against the Jews.

'I was feeling so helpless,' she said, 'and Ruth had just adopted two little boys who had come over on a Children's Transport. Much as I should like to have done the same, my small flat and my demanding job made it quite impossible for me to look after two young children. I was sitting talking to my mother about all this, when the phone rang and Mother answered it. It was a Rickmansworth town councillor, an old friend of my parents. He was ringing to ask Mrs Stern if she knew of any fund which could help a Jewish refugee girl of fourteen, due to leave her elementary school in the summer and worth educating further.

'It came like an answer to a question,' said Lucy. 'Here, I thought, was *my* chance to do something for someone who had suffered under Hitler.'

It seems that Auntie, who was on various committees, had approached the councillor, who had not only *promised* to make enquiries, but had actually *done* so. Kathleen, though delicate, then had walked the long way up Long Lane to Little Hill to discuss the whole matter. Lucy had been a little apprehensive lest the Convent convert me to Catholicism, but the Mother Superior had assured her that there would be no interference with my beliefs. The idea was that Lucy was going to pay for my school fees, my uniform, books and school extras, as well as giving me my pocket-money of sixpence a week, which was later raised to a shilling.

During the holidays Lotte and I were invited to Sunday dinner at Little Hill, Miss Stern's parents' house in Heronsgate. We set off early, because it was a long way up Long Lane, through fields and woodland, and we did not want to be late. It was a beautiful warm summer's day. Heronsgate was then a tiny place in the countryside with large country houses, well separated from each other by spacious gardens and belts of trees. A small lane brought us to the gates of Little Hill, and a lawn with old trees led up to the house. On the terrace lay a man in a deckchair, his long legs stretched out before him, an old-fashioned straw hat on his head, the Sunday paper in his lap, fast asleep.

We hesitated, but almost at once Miss Stern, whom we were told to call Lucy, and a smiling, plump little lady, her mother, came through the french windows to greet us. They made us warmly welcome, showed us over the garden, introduced us to a little dog and woke up 'Father'. Dr Stern got up hurriedly, a little bewildered and not quite sure who we were.

'Something to do with Lucy, are you? That's good, that's good. How are you?' he said.

I felt as though he had far weightier things to concern himself with. He was a very silent, but very polite man with bright blue eyes and a silver shock of hair – a tall, stately man. Lucy told us that he was a scientist, now retired.

Mrs Stern, on the other hand, was a bright, motherly, chatty person. She seemed to be cherished and protected by the whole family, like some delicate Victorian lady, still unfamiliar with the wicked ways of the world. She had brought seven children into the world: two sons and five daughters, but there was still an air of innocence about her.

'We won't tell Mother, it would only upset her,' Lucy and her sisters would often say about some quite trivial business. But it was worthwhile preserving Mrs Stern's peace of mind, if that lay behind her cheerfulness and her kindness.

When we sat down to dinner at the large dining table, I couldn't make out where all the people had suddenly come from. There were nine of us: the whole Stern family was present except for the two doctor brothers.

The family likeness was very marked. All the girls, except Connie, who had flowing black hair and a challenging gaze, had smooth, shining faces, twinkling eyes, short hair parted on the left, and the remarkable gift of being able to speak perfectly clearly with their mouths almost shut, and lips barely moving. This was quite disconcerting when they were together, because one had to watch very carefully to see who was actually speaking.

All of them, apart from the two English teachers, Lucy and Ruth, were scientists, engaged in important war-work. Ruth, the eldest, and Lucy had been among the pioneer women students at Girton in the 1920s. All the 'girls' were then unmarried.

Gradually we became friends of the family and occasionally visited them, first at Little Hill and then at a new house called Broadfields. (Heronsgate, Little Hill, Broadfields – I always associate Lucy with places with lovely names.) The first time I went to Broadfields, one Easter, the garden was a breathtaking sight: I opened the gate and the whole green lawn was swirling with waves of daffodils; a green, astringent scent filled the air. Lucy loved quoting from the poets, particularly from 'Will', as she affectionately called Shakespeare, whose birthday she shared. But Wordsworth's poem about the ten thousand daffodils at a glance must have been written to describe a garden such as at Broadfields.

Lucy had originally hoped to have me with her in Stroud and attend her own school. But the insurmountable obstacle was that Lotte and I did not want to be parted. To my surprise the Salmons seemed not to want to lose me either, and everyone could see the necessity of Lotte's and my remaining together. Lucy very generously forewent the satisfaction (which might not have been as real as she hoped) of day-to-day involvement with my upbringing. She nevertheless hoped I would think of her as a godparent and she certainly always tried hard to act the part of one.

She had wanted me to be brought up in the Jewish faith and was disappointed that I should, in fact, be going to a convent school. As a compromise it was arranged that Lotte and I should have private instruction from a rabbi in Denham each week. Later Kathleen 'examined' the rabbi and decided on the basis of her studies of Catholicism, that he was an unsatisfactory exponent of Judaism, so the instruction was discreetly stopped. I can't pretend that Lotte or I felt this as a great deprivation.

Looking back, I can see that Lucy gave very unselfishly and never demanded gratitude. She always played the part of fairy godmother and has subsequently taken a keen interest in all the various stages of my life. She has always been, and still is, a friend. But I sometimes wonder if she realizes that she had a lucky escape when I did not come to live with her, to upset her ordered way of life.

On the occasions when I spent holidays with Lucy, both in Stroud and Devon, I think I must often have horrified her by my unpunctuality and carelessness and by my inability to appreciate the value of money. I was not a natural 'saver' and enjoyed spending, whereas Lucy, while very generous, was extremely careful to put her money to the best uses. I, who had the benefit of this, could see the force of her argument, and often tried hard, without much success.

I have to thank her for my early interest in Shakespeare, for she took us to Stratford-on-Avon later in our acquaintance and her enthusiasm for Stratford itself and for the plays was infectious. I think she must have been a good teacher and prided herself on being able 'to quell the class with one glance'. Sometimes when she looked at me reprovingly, I could well understand this.

Kathleen was pleased that I was going to St Joan of Arc's. She herself was a Catholic convert, very devout and unswerving in her faith and self-discipline. Of course, she knew the priest, Father Evariste, who knew the nuns, and so it was arranged that I should go and meet the headmistress, Mother Fulbert, during the summer holidays, before the term started. Kathleen came with me.

The convent was a solid, red brick building standing in large grounds on the outskirts of Rickmansworth. In the forecourt a more than life-size statue of St Joan of Arc in full armour brandished a sword at all visitors.

While we were waiting in the entrance hall for Mother Fulbert to arrive, I was struck by the silence. The furniture and staircase gleamed and there was a smell of wax polish. All the brass was shining too and there was a bowl of fresh flowers on the mahogany table. High up on the wall there hung a large wooden cross with Christ nailed to it, his head drooping and blood spurting from the flesh. I was both fascinated and horrified by the sight. A beautiful little statue of the Virgin Mary in a sky-blue gown with a golden halo stood in one of the cornices and some flowers had been placed beside her. The sun slanted in through a high window and fell on to the red patterned carpet. I quite liked the hushed atmosphere; it wasn't like a school at all.

Suddenly there swept through the swing doors a dark shape in flowing black folds – Mother Fulbert!

Her size impressed me: she was large and her voluminous, flowing habit did not help. Her bosom, into which a silver cross was tucked, seemed one unbifurcated expanse, and her face, what one could see of it, was pale and plump with dark bushy eyebrows. A tight white band was stretched across her forehead and a stiff white coif projected several inches all round her face, almost like blinkers. It all looked very hot and uncomfortable. In vain I looked for her hands, but they were concealed somewhere in the drapery, probably one up each sleeve.

She was friendly but business-like and I felt that she didn't much approve of me, though she was very respectful to Kathleen. Most of the time she ignored me, but I was told various rules and Kathleen was given a long list of articles for my school uniform, for which Lucy was going to pay. I had never had a school uniform before; nothing of the sort existed in Germany. This one consisted of a wine-red gym-slip to hang the prescribed fifteen inches from the ground, a cream-coloured shirt, black and maroon tie and black stockings and shoes for winter. There was also a black velour hat with hatband 'to be worn outside at all times when in school uniform'!

For summer we had to have a thoroughly impractical cream-coloured cotton dress with maroon collar and cuffs, a maroon blazer, brown shoes and white ankle socks and a straw hat, 'to be worn at all times . . . etc'. The blazer badge had a Fleur de Lys with the motto: *Fidelis ad Mortem*. I felt like a character out of *The Secret Seven*.

15 The Convent

Being taught by nuns was strange at first and calling them Mother was particularly difficult to get used to. I had romantic notions of the religious vocation, but soon saw that reality was different.

The nuns were never idle. When not teaching they were praying. Mother Fulbert might pace between the desks, murmuring over her Missal, or counting her beads, but she was neither blinkered by her excessive wimple, nor lost in her conversation with the deity. If one were intrepid enough to chat to one's neighbour, she was very quick to swoop despite her bulk. I had thought of nuns as something remote and saintly, but to see 'Fully' at morning assembly was to realize that they could switch quickly from the celestial to the terrestrial plane. She would wander between the ranks of girls and, without interrupting her prayer, would shoot out her hand to cuff someone talking. Before the culprit had recovered from her surprise, Mother Fulbert had said another three 'Hail Marys' and was belabouring another miscreant at the other side of the hall.

At assembly we were often called on to pray in response to requests from local people. Mother Fulbert would read out a letter, sometimes containing a story of real misfortune: 'Mrs X asks us to say five 'Hail Marys' for her son's recovery . . .' she would conclude, and two hundred times five 'Hail Marys' would duly be offered up. I often wondered how the exact number of 'Hail Marys' was decided on. Girls told me that usually people sent in donations with their requests, so perhaps it depended on the size of the offering, or perhaps it may have had more to do with the current demand for prayers and the time available at assembly.

I soon came to realize that under their black serge habits the nuns were human with individual foibles like the rest of us. Mother Madeleine, the music teacher, was very pretty and wore her habit with an air, very erect and poised. She had pink cheeks, pretty teeth, laughed a lot and was always exclaiming 'Fancy!' with a slightly critical intonation. I thought she was the most worldly of our nuns, because sometimes she would send pupils out for cream buns. She also had favourites and, I felt, curried favour with Mother Fulbert. Sometimes she gaily hitched up her skirts and played a good game of tennis, tossing her head like a young, blinkered horse. Me she had given up as a singer quite early on. Shaking her head sadly she would say, 'You haven't much of an ear for music have you, Hanna? Just fancy! And you coming from Germany too. Just fancy!'

Mother Gabriel, the only nun who actually came from France, taught French and spoke English with a very strong accent, dropping all her aitches. She was a good and conscientious teacher, very pale, kind and gentle. She herself was rather bullied by Mother Fulbert and often seemed to be in trouble.

'My *pauvre* 'anna,' she would say to me, 'I weep for you, I pray for you – I too am exile 'ere. I 'ave dear brother in German prison camp,' and she would indeed weep over me. I found her sympathy very comforting and made good progress in French.

Mother Mechtilda taught maths and in spite of my devotion to Mr Rowland it turned out that I was very far behind. In fact, I don't think I ever quite caught up. Certainly to begin with half the time I did not know what it was all about. Mother Mechtilda, a young, shy nun with chilblains and often with cracked lips, was sweetly resigned to my inadequacy.

Mother Clodoald taught art. No one quite knew how old she was, but she was generally believed to be in her seventies and we felt that she should have retired years ago. She was forever muttering and complaining about everything and everybody, and whereas I had enjoyed art classes at Mill End, here we were forever having to draw 'patterns'.

The only member of staff who seemed beyond human weakness was the Reverend Mother Superior, Mother Septima,

143

whom we rarely saw. I was called into the presence only three or four times, and always found her sitting like a small, wrinkled bushbaby, because the large, round, dark-tinted glasses she wore dominated her little face. She was always calm and serene, no doubt looking 'quite through the deeds of men'. I was in awe of her, but thought her very fair and good. She had been at St Joan's for nearly fifty years by the time I arrived.

The other subjects were taught by lay teachers. My favourite was Miss Leach, who taught English and history. She was young, beautifully dressed and a stimulating teacher. She took endless trouble to correct all my mistakes in English grammar and must have helped my progress with the language a great deal. Certainly she infected me with her love of Wordsworth. For a time she wore an engagement ring and we all detected a far-away look in her eyes. But alas for our dream of romance! One day the ring disappeared, and with it the far-away look.

I loved writing compositions and vied with a girl called Sylvia Broad to see who could write the most. Poor Miss Leach! I had a very fertile imagination and would deluge her with interminable romantic yarns. The best essays were always read aloud to the class by their authors, and whenever I was called upon to read, the class would settle back in happy anticipation. No doubt they appreciated my extravagant sense of moral drama, but more than that, they enjoyed hearing my funny accent. Once I was so lacking in foresight as to have written, '. . . and the wicked witch vanished in a cloud of white vapour', which emerged as: '. . . and ze vicked vitch wanished in a cloud of vite wapour'. The class roared and even Miss Leach could not repress a smile.

'Please Miss, could Hanna read the story to us *again*?' It was all very good-natured.

But I don't think Mother Fulbert ever really liked me. She was a very competent headmistress and had a great deal to do. She was in many ways a good woman, certainly, but she could be terribly unfair and unjust, particularly to those who were not in a position to retaliate. And she had her favourites, both among the pupils and the nuns. Mother Madeleine with her pretty ways and light laughter did much as she pleased, whereas poor timid Mother Gabriel was often bullied and even shouted at by Mother Fulbert in front of the class. She always received these attacks humbly, but she obviously suffered under them and sometimes she arrived in class with red-rimmed eyes.

As far as I was concerned, the fact that Fully taught arithmetic did not help. It was my worst subject, which she soon discovered. Many a time she called me out to the blackboard and, flustered by her chivvying, I soon became unable to do the simplest thing. I felt she enjoyed my discomfiture. She would often remind me of how grateful I ought to be to Kathleen, sometimes threatening that she would tell her of this or that minor misdemeanour. I was permanently in dread of her sharp tongue or thunderous anger, and only too glad that I was not a boarder. I kept out of her way as much as possible. For one incident I never forgave her.

It was one of Kathleen's rules that we had to make our beds before leaving for school. On this occasion I was late in getting up, scrambled into my clothes, dashed down a cup of tea and was out of the house like a whirlwind, so as not to be late.

During assembly Mother Fulbert called me out before the whole school and told everybody that my kind guardian had just rung up, most distressed, because I had not made my bed and asking for me to be sent straight back home to see to it. I stood in front of the whole school while Mother Fulbert pointed at me, the ungrateful child who had everything given to her and who could not even be bothered to make her own bed. She was so eloquent in her wrath that for the moment I actually felt quite wicked and guilty. I hurried back home, weeping and breathless, towards the terrible doom – perhaps banishment – for which Mother Fulbert had prepared me. At the same time I felt angry at Muriel for telling on me and at Kathleen for bringing the school into it, and I hated Mother Fulbert for her cruelty. I swore I would never go back to school.

Back at home I got a lengthy dressing-down from Kathleen, who reminded me of all the work Muriel had to do for us and how thoughtless it was of me not even to help her in little ways.

'What a disgrace having to call you back from school. Now go down instantly and make your bed and don't let this sort of thing ever happen again!' Afterwards Kathleen told me to hurry back to school. In tears I told her that I could *never* go back to school after what had happened, and I related the story of the assembly incident. I think even Kathleen felt a little horrified at the extreme reactions her phone call had produced.

In fact I did not go back to school that day, but played truant. I went for a long walk, contemplating the most terrible alternatives: suicide, running away . . .

In the afternoon I met friends (Janet Houghton and Valerie Gibbons) coming back from school. They wanted to know what had happened at home, and in turn they told me how Mother Fulbert had gone on about me even after I had left the hall. They were utterly disgusted at Fully's behaviour and full of sympathy for me. They said they never made their beds and how *awful* of Kathleen to ring up Fully!

'Catch my mother doing that!'

That was all very comforting. I allowed myself to be persuaded not to run away or kill myself. Later, like 'ze vicked vitch', the incident became a friendly tease.

'Hanna, have you made your bed today?' I would be greeted by friends on the way to school.

Oddly enough the episode had made me something of a heroine. My scrapes, my accent, my untameable hair and my fantastic imaginings were evidently welcomed as a relief from the monotony of school life, and I began to make friends and find life much more tolerable.

I was fully aware of my good fortunes and of the kindness and generosity that Lotte and I had met with. At the same time I was never allowed to forget that it behoved me to be good and grateful, and that I owed life a debt. Perhaps I was oversensitive about it. But it never seemed to occur to Mother Fulbert, Kathleen, or Auntie, when they reminded me of how lucky I was and how I must see to it that I deserved my good fortune, that I was in fact deeply conscious of the kindness I had received and that my misdemeanours were not due to ingratitude, but to adolescent thoughtlessness. In fact, these constant reminders had the reverse effect and clouded my feelings of gratitude with a certain resentment.

While writing this, I discovered among some old exercise books a few *Herzensausbrüche* (outpourings from the heart), which seem to have served the purpose of getting grouses and grumbles and feelings of unjust treatment off my chest, even though no one else ever saw them.

One such outpouring is dated 6 September 1940 – the holidays just before I was due to start at the Convent; it was still written in the double cypher of German and Gothic script:

Today I see once again the difference between parents scolding one and strangers being cross. Today I really hated

Kathleen! I am tired of having to be beholden and to behave like a model of virtue all the time! How I wish I were grown up and standing on my own feet! I wish too that I could just very quickly have a good cry out in Mummy's lap. Everywhere I feel that I am an unwelcome burden and that everyone would be glad to be rid of me.

Today it is such a glorious day outside with golden sunshine and a burnished blue sky and I have to moulder away here, in my room underground ALL DAY! But I am not admitting my error. I know I am sulking and feeling sorry for myself, but I also feel that my punishment is unjust. I don't think I have to take everything lying down, not even from Miss High and Mighty: Miss Kathleen Salmon! I don't suppose she was a saint at my age. And I wasn't even naughty.

What happened was this: when the siren went this morning, instead of going down into the shelter-room, I went outside to ask Muriel (who must have told Kathleen, the old tell-tale) whether the siren had really gone, or whether it was a false alarm. A perfectly genuine question, as the children from next door had not come across, as they usually do when there's an air-raid. I did stay in the garden a bit after that, and suddenly K came storming towards me like a Fury, screaming, 'Go downstairs *at once*! I shall see you in a minute!' But she kept me waiting in anxious apprehension for quite a while, before bursting into my room, eyes bulging, shouting brusquely: 'I won't put up with you and your naughtinesses any longer; I've had enough of you! You are not fit to go to the Convent. I am not going to send a naughty girl there! You are utterly in disgrace and confined to your room all day and you are not to leave it except to go to the toilet, (how kind, I thought bitterly) and no more of your tricks!'

And then she started all over again. I tried to make my excuses and apologies, but she wouldn't listen to them and with a look that could kill, she left the room, banging the door behind her, leaving me behind, trembling with suppressed rage, confused and miserable. But having had time to think about it, I don't feel one spark of remorse – why indeed? He who sits in a glass house shouldn't throw stones! When the siren goes, Kathleen is the first to go outside aeroplane-spotting. And most ironic of all, yesterday when the alarm went, she actually told us to go outside and play in the garden;

that it was a false alarm. Today she says the opposite. It's just her moodiness. I never know where I am. As she went up the stairs I heard her call out to Muriel, 'Hanna is in disgrace all day; she is not to leave her room. Will you tell me if she does?'

'Yes, Miss Kathleen,' was Muriel's triumphant answer.

So here I sit with my feelings. Actually, now that I have simmered down, it's not so bad; at any rate, I can do some work without being interrupted by Auntie all the time asking me to run messages. On the other hand, today I had intended to go blackberrying and to take my tea with me. It's such a heavenly day! But there will be other heavenly days and I can go another time.

So why am I beginning to cry? Anger? Obstinacy? Self-pity? I think if anyone came near me now, I should decapitate them. In moments like these my homesickness for Mummy and Daddy comes welling up, and tears do help a little. I suppose this is my fate and I have to bear it. What a hard fate is mine!

Actually I feel a lot better now, having got my feelings down on paper.

These isolated incidents did not prevent me from being happy at home and at school and making some very good friends. Among them were two very different characters, Valerie Gibbons and Janet Houghton, both of whom lived nearby.

Valerie was the youngest of five girls, brought up by a widowed mother. The eldest was already married and Valerie was about to become an aunt. One sister was in the WRENS, another was about to join the WAAFS, a third had just got engaged. All five girls were extremely vital and beautiful. Valerie was very impressive: she was taller than me with a much more developed figure and an admirable dress-sense. The belt of her gym-slip was always drawn very tight to emphasize her narrow waist and the fullness below and above. Her long, brown hair was worn loose with a madonna parting and she refused to wear her school hat, but carried it rolled up in her hand, ready to shove on the back of her head at the sight of Fully. She had wonderful white teeth and a wide, infectious smile that narrowed her blue-grey eyes into cheeky slits. She even wore delicate touches of lipstick.

She was a very extroverted and happy-go-lucky sort of person and through her older sisters knew many of the answers to questions that puzzled me. She was perfectly at ease with boys and didn't go in for violent crushes. She had started her periods long ago and her frank talk was the only preparation I had for the first arrival of mine. Kathleen referred to sexual matters only through analogy with birds and bees.

Janet was quite different. She was a year younger than we were and still quite slight. She was sensitive and not yet very self-confident, but she was a warm and very responsive person. She was very good at arithmetic and maths and always ready to help me with them. And since essay-writing came hard to her, she was gratifyingly appreciative of my story-telling.

In the mornings she sometimes called for me. 'Have you made up any more of your story?' And so, on the way to school I would relate the next instalment of my romantic tales.

One day she asked me home to tea with her after school and that was the start of a life-long friendship, not only with Janet, but with the entire Houghton family.

I was very happy with the Salmons, but it was a formal household. Both Kathleen and Auntie, though kind and dear, were naturally reserved people who often recoiled in horror before my sudden onslaughts of affection: 'Hanna, don't be so gushing!' or, 'Now then, Hanna, not so wild, learn to control yourself.'

I am sure it was very good for me to learn how to control my feelings. But the Houghtons were less stiff and never shocked by my behaviour. Of course, they didn't have the responsibility of bringing us up, but, as a result, I felt there I could let my hair down and be more myself, doing daft things with Janet and Janet's sister, Liz, and other friends, without being reprimanded.

Mrs Houghton was a free-thinking, broad-minded person with a wonderful capacity for talking and listening. Everyone there seemed to think of me as someone rather special, my odd ways and ideas were something to be admired, and so I felt worthwhile and appreciated, and my feelings of guilt, or of disappointing Kathleen's high expectations of me, were allayed.

I remember we spent the first weekend away from Colne House with the Houghtons. It was to be a special birthday treat for Janet. Lotte and I were to be collected by Mr Houghton, Janet and Liz, and together we were going to see *The Corsican Brothers* at the Odeon, with Douglas Fairbanks Jr in a double role, and he was my hero! We were to return to their house,

Tyburn Way, for a birthday tea, stay overnight and not return home till Sunday evening. It was the most fantastic treat to which I had been looking forward ever since we had been invited.

But little did Mr Houghton realize what it meant to invite 'enemy aliens' overnight. Auntie told him that we had to have police permission to spend the night away from home, even though the Houghtons lived no more than fifteen minutes away.

'Leave it to me,' he said briskly and led us down to the police station there and then. While the four of us waited anxiously outside, Mr Houghton, in his best military manner as a First World War Captain of Infantry, marched into the police station. He emerged quite soon, dapper and smiling, 'Come along girls, it's going to be all right.'

'Can we stay? Is it all right?' We eagerly pressed to know what had been said.

'Stuff and nonsense! Ridiculous nonsense! They've got to get in touch with headquarters in London and we have to come back after the pictures to find out if permission has been granted. Two little things like you! Never mind, it'll be all right.'

Lotte started crying and the rest of us felt on tenter-hooks until we gave ourselves up to *The Corsican Brothers*, which exceeded all my expectations: Douglas Fairbanks leapt and flew, fought duels, flashed his teeth and rescued damsels in distress, so that I had quite forgotten about our own uncertain fate.

And when we returned, the police said it was quite in order. We were over the moon and somehow the suspense had turned the whole thing into a marvellous adventure. All the way home Mr Houghton burst out chuckling every now and then, mumbling to himself, 'What a ridiculous bit of nonsense!'

Joyously we went back through the black-out to a warm and glowing Tyburn Way, where Mrs Houghton had been busy piling the tea-table high with cakes and sandwiches, jellies and trifles. Lotte and I were treated with particular indulgence and attention, our presence there having been so hard won. We had great fun playing games and larking about in bed and chatting late into the night.

Mr Houghton brought us a cup of tea in bed next day, we sang and played and had no letters to deliver! It was like a real holiday and we were happy and tired when Mr Houghton returned us personally on Sunday evening to Colne House.

Auntie gave us birthday parties too. Lotte's in the summer was conducive to outdoor games in the garden, but mine was in winter and indoors. Kathleen always enjoyed helping us arrange the games and prizes and she went to endless trouble devising the most splendid treasure hunts through a large part of the rambling house and all the clues consisted of enigmatic little verses made up by herself. It was the highlight of the occasion, vying only with Muriel's splendid spread of jellies, trifles and lovely cakes, and the large lounge was a wonderful place for games, with a log fire roaring in the grate.

Auntie and Kathleen certainly made good use of that room. As one of her contributions to the war effort, Auntie, who loved playing bridge, arranged large bridge parties in the lounge, once every month or so, with the proceeds going to some benevolent fund or other. There were ten to twelve tables, each set out with crisp packs of cards, scoring pads and pencils sharpened by us.

The 'bridge ladies' always amazed me. Seen *en masse* they seemed a distinct breed of human being. Many of them were middle-aged and brought with them an air of decorum and opulent gentility that hung fragrantly around their fur coats, even after they had been taken off. Their twin sets matched their tweed skirts; strings of pearls lay around their necks and some of them wore flashing rings in rows of three, one on top of the other. Their hair was groomed, their nails manicured and tinted.

They were smilingly polite, but went to their tables with an eagerness that was beyond my comprehension, to sit through the long afternoon with rapt concentration, nimbly shuffling and dealing and silently playing their cards. When I handed round the thin paste-and-cress sandwiches, or Muriel's little iced cakes, they asked me about school in friendly, somewhat strangulated voices and I noticed how the aggressive red lipstick, fashionable in those days, sometimes seemed to bleed over the edges of their mouths, and how the pale powder lay on their skins, smelling very agreeably.

In fact, many of the 'bridge ladies' did not spend much of their time at cards. They regularly shed their furs and donned their uniforms and were busy in all sorts of good works connected with the war. Their untiring vigour was the backbone of the WVS and similar organizations.

Kathleen's musical concerts were something very different

from the bridge parties, although they served similar good causes. For them the two Bechstein grands were tuned and Kathleen conspired with Avril Leventon, a close friend since their Academy days, to organize the programme. A number of professional musicians, many of whom had also been fellow students, lived in or near Rickmansworth at that time. Muriel Middleton, the contralto, Richard Ford, the tenor, Esther Hulbert, Sybil Evers, the opera singer and wife of Harold Abrahams, and Esther Rixon are some of those whose names I remember.

The lounge held seventy to eighty people comfortably. Lotte and I helped to set out the hired chairs, and in the evening we became the 'ushers', feeling terribly important. And, of course, we were allowed to stay and listen to the concerts and during the intervals we helped to pass round the refreshments.

As time passed, the concerts became quite well-known and it was impossible to find room for everyone who wanted to come. Kathleen ranged wider for her artists and there were memorable evenings with Phyllis Sellick and Cyril Smith on the two grands, Colin Sauer, a young and promising violinist, and Angel Grandi, a Spanish violinist who played some wonderful duets with Kathleen at the piano.

Kathleen still played a great deal at that time. I loved to watch her thin, strong fingers as they hovered and flew. She was particularly fond of Mozart, Chopin and Debussy, which she played with a delicacy of touch and a clarity of phrasing, so that often I drifted to sleep at night through ripples of water and touches of breezes.

One Christmas Kathleen and her closest friends put on *The Beggar's Opera* in costume. It was almost a family affair and even Lotte and I had small parts. I thought the finest contribution to that hilarious occasion was made by Harold Abrahams; he had a good, deep voice and sang and acted, as he did everything else, with great enthusiasm and relish. He was easily my favourite among that group of friends. I knew nothing about his past as an Olympic athlete and gold medallist; here he was simply the husband of Sybil Evers. But I was bowled over by this conspicuously tall, spontaneous person. He would seize me when he came into the lounge, whirl me round and ask about school and my ambitions, as if he really thought that I mattered. His wartime post with the Ministry of Economic Warfare did not always allow him to get away to the Colne House concerts, but whenever his wife, Sybil Evers, was performing, he always came. He was very proud of her. When she died of cancer some years later, he was quite shattered. She was a sweet and gentle person, and he made everyone with whom he came in contact seem a little more alive.

With the occupation of Belgium in the early summer of 1940 my parents could no longer write to us, but could only send messages to my relations at Hampstead through the International Red Cross.

In the last letters that did reach us around Easter 1940 my father scolds us for not writing more often. They had not heard from us for over a month. The new school year would have started and they did not know what was happening.

As for our American business, that doesn't look too hopeful at the moment, as the papers necessary from Uncle Max and Walter have not yet arrived. It will probably take another six months before everything is arranged and then a few more months before you will be able to join us, and so we must all of us still have a great deal of patience. It is therefore all the more important that you should write to us at least once a fortnight, otherwise I am consumed too much with homesickness for you and will get old more quickly. You ask, dear Hannele, whether I am still so young. No, my dear child, I miss you two and your youth. Am I to run down the hills of the *Gerresheimer Schweiz* by myself, or look for Easter eggs in the *Lebkuchenbaum*? Or on walks talk to myself and tell myself stories of what the countryside looked like 100,000 years ago?

But it was wonderful that we spent your childhood days so companionably – and so we shall continue when we are together again. And now I must ask you urgently to answer Mummy's questions in her last letter to you about your schooling. *Under no circumstances* must you, dear Hannele, be without a *regular* daily routine . . .

My mother had had her thirty-ninth birthday:

. . . and your loving birthday letters arrived almost three weeks early, so early that I hoped and more than half-expected that there would be another letter from you for my birthday, which I am sad to say didn't happen. Therefore on the morning of my birthday Daddy once more handed out your letters, and once more I re-read them. It was only during dinner, after the delicious soup cooked by Oma, during the usual short delay before the next course, that Daddy read to me your *truly lovely poem* that he had kept back, dear Hannele. . . . Do try and send me a photograph of you both – I wait for them with *such longing* . . . And now I hope we'll have a letter from you this week, otherwise Daddy's face will grow longer and longer. It is almost a year since you left us. Do you think of that too?

16 Complex Relationships

Kathleen Salmon played an important role in my life. When I first met her I thought her very beautiful – not pretty, but with a serene, classical beauty. She looked at one very directly and seriously with her wide-open, grey eyes, which could be disconcerting. Her pale face might have been carved out of ivory; with her fine, slightly aquiline nose it was almost the face of a young warrior. Her dark hair, short and glossy, was worn with a centre parting and fell away on either side in soft waves. She had arching eyebrows and a delicate forehead which she sometimes puckered into fine lines. Her lips were thin and sensitive and when she laughed her whole face became animated. She was tall and over-slender, very graceful, moving like a long-legged water-bird. In her younger photographs, when her cheeks were fuller and her hair lay looped in earphones, she looked a lovely, merry girl, not as transparently spiritual as she now appeared. When we came into her orbit she was about thirty-two or three.

She was a complex, enigmatic person. Her asthma was mysterious in its origins and strange in its behaviour, but it killed her at the age of forty-three. We were told that the illness made its first appearance when she was about fourteen after a cold caught at the school swimming baths. At first it was only occasional and not very severe. It worsened; specialists were consulted, allergies investigated – there was even a period in Switzerland. From all accounts she was able to lead a fairly normal life most of the time during her late teens and early twenties. She studied the piano at the Royal Academy of Music and started on what seemed a very promising career as a concert pianist under the stage name of Sarah Salmon.

In the thirties she went to Spain, whether for health or professional reasons, I don't know, but the climate of Malaga and Seville suited her so well that she stayed in the South for several years. She spoke Spanish fluently when we knew her. She was very happy there. There were photographs of her in a flaring Spanish dress mounted side-saddle at the Fiesta of Seville, and others of her swirling with castanets and big jangling earrings, laughing happily. The whole way of life seemed to draw her out.

We learnt that she had fallen in love there with a young Spanish lawyer who wanted to marry her. I could never quite understand why she didn't. Kathleen did not speak about him much, but Auntie once told me that she had decided that it wasn't fair to marry because of her illness, for she felt it obliged her never to have children. To me it seemed a strange sacrifice, particularly as the young man was fully aware of the illness and continued to write, even after she returned home, begging her to come back and marry him. I thought of my cousin Margot, who had taken the opposite course and found happiness, however short.

One other thing happened in Spain which had the most profound effect on Kathleen's whole life. She became a Roman Catholic. To her conventionally C of E family this was quite a shock. Auntie gradually came to accept it, for she loved Kathleen very much, but I don't think her father or her brother ever did, and it drove a wedge between her and them.

Had she become a Catholic because of the young lawyer? I asked Auntie one day.

'No,' said Auntie, 'Kathleen claims she had a vision.'

Kathleen herself refused to elaborate on her vision, or revelation, or whatever it was. Of course, the whole idea intrigued and fascinated me and my imagination filled in the gaps.

Kathleen had been in Spain during the Civil War and had not been home many months when we first met her. It must have been very hard for her to find herself back at home in wartime Britain, with her devoted suitor, her Spanish friends and the sun of the South mere memories. Unable to pursue her career, distanced from her family, except her mother, her life must have seemed rather aimless. It was partly to give her some responsibility and direction that Auntie 'got us for Kathleen' to take her mind off things and to give her something to do. And Kathleen took our upbringing very seriously indeed, sometimes a little too seriously, supervising not only our baths, but all our tasks and daily routine.

I admired her very much and grew to love her dearly. The only trouble was that, because of her own unsettled state, Kathleen sometimes gave way to moods and her reaction to our inevitable misdemeanours was not consistent. Sometimes she went off the deep end over minor things, such as failing to wash one's hands, or being unpunctual, at other times she was very reasonable and fair. Often we got what we affectionately called 'lectures' on how to behave properly, especially on self-restraint and not getting too demonstrative or excited.

Although her training was often irksome, we doubtless bene-fited from it in many ways. Not only did we learn not to use a knife when eating an omelette, how to deal with a globe artichoke, how to prepare grapefuit and how to lay the table for a five-course dinner (largely an academic exercise during the war), but Kathleen also tried to improve our English and widen our horizons. To that end she sometimes invoked the help of Esther Hulbert (from the converted consulting-room flat) and together we would read through Shakespeare's plays. We enjoyed this, although we understood little at first. Probably one of the first words that intrigued me, because Kathleen refused to explain it, was the word 'whore', which I pronounced 'vore'. On Saturdays or during holidays Kathleen gave us general knowledge com-petitions or vocabulary tests with little prizes. In these ways, in transcribing books into braille for the blind, in playing the piano and in reading travel biographies from Boots library she spent her days.

By now the last direct letter from my parents was more than a year old, and the little Red Cross message acknowledging with relief the news that I was going to a Secondary High School was the last direct contact Lotte and I had had with them. I kept my hope strong with daily bargains made with God that if I were good and honest and brave, then he would reward us with a return of Mummy and Daddy. I could not and would not allow myself to doubt, although my nights were often disturbed by troubling dreams and lurid imaginings. Those sixty letters and postcards I had, all sent between the day of our departure in May '39 and April '40, I read and re-read.

Occasionally complicated instructions arrived from Tante Rosel telling us how to write to our parents via America in a guarded way, as though they were distant relatives.

I should so much like it, my dear girls, [she wrote in early 1941 from a nursing home] that your dear parents could get some *direct* communication from you. It might be a good idea if you were to write a letter in German to your Uncle Max in America, addressing the letter to him and telling him your news. Tell him that you are well and how you are getting on at school and that you are doing well, and that you are often invited to tea-parties by friends. Only don't use the word 'tea-party' – it sounds so English. And don't say 'Mummy' or 'Daddy' and don't ask whether they will be coming to America soon. Write instead, 'How are you, dear Else, are you well? And you, dear Adölf, are you still keeping your spirits up and keeping active mentally? You would both be surprised to see how tall the two of us have got . . .' roughly on those lines. You see, it must not look as though these letters were coming from England via America to Germany, because that is not allowed and all the letters are censored, and then they would be returned. Discuss it with Mrs Salmon or Miss Salmon and they will help you. Then send the letter to Egon so that he can make sure that it is all right. You might start the letter with 'My dear ones'.

Don't forget Inge's birthday on Saturday. It is so difficult for her just now, particularly as I'm not at home to keep the house going, and I am so low in health. Ask your Doctor Salmon if there is anything that will cure nerve-trouble and give one sleep without pills and restore one's courage in life.

Next Sunday I shall be returning home, and I pray God to give me strength to run my home and not to fall a burden to my children. If only Max would send a little extra money again, so that I might see a specialist and be able to take a little more care of myself – the doctors are so expensive; but poor Max now has to find the money to help to get your dear parents out and to America. It takes many thousands of dollars – and I hope that *this* time something will come of it.

[Another letter:] My foot is still no better. I was so hoping to be able to get a permit to visit you. But the wound won't heal and the doctor who came to see me yesterday looked at the wound and said that I mustn't walk about the house, but that I have to lie down. I have already been lying down for five weeks without any improvement. I can't bear all this lying down by myself much longer, it makes me really nervous. I lie there all day thinking of my dear Ala and of your dear father and I long for them so much. I am sending you a little postal order: Christmas is coming and you will be wanting to buy Christmas presents for the Salmons. But with all our doctor's bills and all the medicines just now, I am sorry not to be sending you more . . .

My poor aunt's leg would not heal up and gave her great pain. It had been troubling her for two years without being properly diagnosed. With all the strains and worries of Ala's death, about my parents, about us, about Kurt and Inge (still unable to marry), her health began to deteriorate, but she toiled on bravely, complaining very little, always trying to cheer us up and comfort us. She now had to negotiate the three flights of stone stairs on all fours, because of the pain in her leg. Finally her trouble was diagnosed as tuberculosis of the bone and she was taken into a nursing home from which she never returned. She had tried to spare us her worries, and it was only now, in these last stages that she let drop hints about how difficult things had become.

Auntie and Kathleen never suggested that we might visit her, though it would have pleased her so much. So I dimly worried about Tante Rosel too, for I was very fond of her and she was so fond of my father and us. She was warm and loving, and when she was well she was full of fun.

I cannot remember that Kathleen ever did in fact help us with those complicated letters to my parents, about which new instructions arrived from my aunt almost every week. Now that direct letters to my parents were no longer possible I became more neglectful of my correspondence, particularly after several of my attempts had been returned by my relatives as too long and too risky for the censors and I suspected that others that I wrote were never sent.

Gradually Kathleen stopped encouraging us to write to or talk about my parents and I soon learnt to keep quiet about my worries and longings. I think Auntie and Kathleen felt that if we were to be assimilated in Britain, the sooner we loosened our silken ties with our old home the better. Many a time Kathleen would say to me, 'Now, English girls would not give vent to their feelings like that. You must learn to control your feelings, Hanna, if you want to be like an English girl.'

And I *did* want to be like an English girl.

On the rare occasions when my poor Tante Rosel came to visit us after obtaining police permission and after a troublesome journey, hobbling from the station with gifts that she could ill-afford, it was all so disappointing. Of course, Tante Rosel was received very politely and given tea, but it was all so stiff and formal and I hated myself for seeing Tante Rosel as she must appear in Kathleen's cool eyes: her limp and her careworn face, her funny accent of which she was quite unaware, the excited manner of her speech and her old-fashioned clothes – all so un-English. And having to speak English all the time was a strain for her. I think we had a little while on our own, but we were ill at ease and must have appeared cold too, embarrassed by her warm, uninhibited ways. I never will forget her face and her quiet tears as we saw her off on the train. But she was contented that we were in good hands and well looked after and happy. I felt torn in all directions afterwards, but did not know how to resolve the conflict. Auntie did say afterwards how much she had liked my aunt, 'poor thing'. Of my cousin, Egon, she was more critical. In fact she discouraged him from coming again, after he whiled away the time waiting for us down by the little river, kissing his fiancée.

Periodically news filtered through from Germany via America telling of complicated negotiations and repeated setbacks. We must be patient; the visas would be issued, the sponsors would yet be found, there was a possible route through Lisbon . . . or Cuba . . . or even by way of the Far East . . .

Uncle Max, perhaps despairing of success, or worried about the possibility of an invasion of Britain, thought we should go to the United States and await our parents there, but we were happy in Rickmansworth and doubtful at the prospect of a vast, unknown America and a barely remembered uncle. Eventually, by circuitous routes, my father was consulted and he replied that if we wanted to stay in England no one should force us to do otherwise. 'You'll be happy with that news, my dears,' wrote Tante Rosel.

Occasionally until the end of 1941 third- or fourth-hand news arrived via America that 'Else and Adolf are well, grandparents too; distressed only at hearing no news of children . . .' Then there was silence. Uncle Max took to sending us philosophical letters full of homely advice, trying to fill the gap.

One afternoon in the spring of 1943 I came home from school and found that tea had been kept for me on the trolley in the sitting-room, an unusual occurrence. Everyone was very nice to me and listened to me as I talked about school. On top of that Kathleen had a little treat for us: a new toothbrush, toothpaste and a flannel for each of us. Presents in those days, even mundane ones, were exciting and would help to spin out my pocket-money too. How sweet of Kathleen!

As tea was cleared away and I was going out to help Muriel, Kathleen said, 'Come and sit down Hanna. I have something to tell both of you. You are going to have to be very brave and grown-up.' She looked at us with those great, serious eyes, full of compassion. And then she told us. A Red Cross letter had eventually reached my relatives via Switzerland, informing them of my father's death in the concentration camp of Lodz in Poland, where he had died of heart failure, on 26 April 1942. That was all. Not a word about my mother.

It seems amazing that I cannot remember what I thought, felt or did. Perhaps it is not so amazing. I don't think I could take it in at the time. They were words; nothing was changed. It was not as though I had seen my father the day before. I had been living with him in my mind for more than three years. I don't think I went to school the next day. The scantiness of the information gnawed away at me and the hope to which I had clung so defiantly was gone. But that realization came to me only gradually.

I remember Mother Gabriel coming over to my desk and starting to say something and then just crying. That set me off too. Kindness – and people were kind – made me cry most easily. For a while I could not bear re-reading my parents' old letters; they made me dissolve into floods of unquenchable tears.

But what I do remember is that with this news there came my nightly broodings and horrible imaginings. Because there were no details I imagined dreadful tortures. I was haunted most of all by the uncertainty of my mother's fate. I visualized my father protesting at some injustice done to a fellow prisoner and then being killed for it brutally by some Nazi devil – died of heart failure? His heart had been as sound as a bell! But where was Mummy? Round and round went the dark, tormenting thoughts, which troubled me for many years. Even now, occasionally, the doubts and uncertainties return to haunt me.

I knew with a certainty and comforted myself with the thought that my father had died with dignity, whatever humiliation or harshness they had put upon him. And the other comfort was that he could not suffer any more. But my young mother, who was not so strong – what of her? I couldn't bear to think of her separated from my father. I kept imagining her large brown eyes filled with fear, and the thought that I should never meet her again kept recurring. My only hope was that she too was dead and safe from further suffering. But she had barely lived!

Lotte and I drew closer together and tried to live as our parents would have wanted us to. They seemed all around us.

After the news of my father's death our standing with the Salmons gradually changed. Nothing was said, but it was accepted that Colne House was our home. I no longer felt that I should be evicted for my misdemeanours. Apart from the death of my father and the now evident fact that we should not be going to the USA, at least, not till after the war, we learnt that Tante Rosel, worn out with illness and sadness, had died. I feel sad that her death did not mean more to us. She had not felt really welcome at Colne House and, of course, her bad leg had made the journey a painful effort and then an impossibility for her. The last months of her life were spent in a nursing home, in great pain and distress. So, to a large extent we had lost touch with her.

Apart from these external changes, Auntie and Kathleen had by now become genuinely fond of us, and warm-hearted Muriel too, accepted us as part of the family despite the extra work we caused. The Salmons even became a little possessive and they may have felt it would be best for us finally to cast off our links with the past.

Perhaps something of that sort was at the back of Kathleen's mind when she came downstairs one day to 'go through our things' and to see what could be spared and given to her Catholic protégé family. Perhaps she was trying to teach us how to be charitable. If so, she was going the wrong way about it. I did try to remonstrate with her when she took my beloved doll, Ruth, who had been with me ever since I was six.

'You are too big for dolls, Hanna, and it's selfish to hang on to toys when you don't need them and other poor children would be grateful for them.'

Kathleen made me feel mean and selfish, but although I had grown out of playing with dolls, how could I tell her that Ruth meant more to me than a mere doll, but was a link with childhood and parents? I think Kathleen did realize that, but felt that these tangible links continued as constant reminders of Mummy and Daddy. I got the feeling that she was a little jealous of our continued longing for our parents, little realizing that it was their very absence that made us treasure every link doubly, and that giving things away made no difference to our feelings, apart from setting up a resentment which I found hard to overcome.

I recalled my father's letter in which he told us how he had selected our favourite toys and books and treasured possessions, and how he had said that some things should stay in the family for later generations, particularly the famous Bavarian doll's house, that had even survived the *Kristallnacht*. That was a family possession, not just a doll's house. I remembered the trouble my parents had packing and unpacking at the customs and how the crate's arrival at Hampstead had been a feast-day. On their visits to us in Rickmansworth my aunt and cousins had lugged our toys piecemeal at our urgent requests.

'Just think of the pleasure you'll give those children who have so little, if you give them your doll's house,' Kathleen said, coming down again to go through 'unnecessary' things. This was too much. Even at the risk of being told that I was selfish and ungrateful I remonstrated with Kathleen and told her that it was a 'family thing', made by a relative. 'I really don't want to part with that.'

'How often do you play with it? Hm? It's just a nuisance standing around here, gathering dust.'

'But I *do* look at it, Kathleen, and it can be for my or Lotte's children.'

However, I couldn't stand up against Kathleen's reminder just how much we had to be grateful for, and how I wasn't even prepared to part with some old toys for needy children in return.

So it went too. Some weeks later it was broken and quite destroyed by rough unfeeling hands. I saw its ruins when I had to accompany Kathleen to deliver some clothes we had grown out of. Ruth too had lost her eyes and a leg. How I longed to pick her up and take her back with me!

I could see no reason for Kathleen's subsequent onslaught on my German books. No one could read them and they were deeply treasured, particularly the set of 'Nesthäckchen' books for which I had pleaded with my father, and which I still re-read occasionally. I can only suppose that Kathleen honestly felt that reminders of childhood and our parents encouraged unhealthy brooding.

Our clothes, too, came under scrutiny. We were growing, of course, and things could not last forever, but it seemed to me that all the care with which Mummy had provided coats and skirts, jumpers and dresses for the future, so that we should be independent and well-dressed without having to be a burden on anyone for years to come, was in vain.

'You have far too many clothes,' Kathleen said, 'you can't possibly wear them all. Think of Enid and Audrey, this would just fit them.'

'But I could still wear it if I let out the turnings and the hem.'

Couldn't Kathleen see that Mummy had not saved and scraped and planned and shopped to clothe the 'adopted' Catholic family, but to save Tante Rosel and Onkel Max expense, and to know that we had decent clothes? I couldn't bear to think of Mummy while Kathleen was sifting through our things. It was my favourite dress with the button-on skirt that was the first to go, though Lotte could have had a lot of wear out of it.

'Lotte will be sick of it, having grown out of her own.' Always Kathleen had a valid argument ready. And so, very soon I had no winter coat to fit me and Auntie had to cut down one of her own. She went to a great deal of trouble to please me, but I could not help regretting the waste of my mother's forethought and extra-long hems. Auntie was very careful never to interfere with Kathleen's decisions, because we were 'her charges'.

But the gifts were not all one way. Kathleen had persuaded Auntie to let Enid, the eldest of the nine Catholic children, work at Colne House, dusting and helping and generally learning how to be a parlour maid. But Enid had lice! It transpired that her whole family had lice and that Enid and her mother had been fully aware of this when Enid came to work for us. We discovered this only after Auntie exclaimed in horror one evening, 'Hanna! What's that crawling in your hair?' There was, in fact, quite a lot crawling in my hair, and in Lotte's too. The mystery was solved next day when we learnt that Enid had used my brush and comb. Auntie sent her home with a note to her mother, explaining the situation and telling her not to come back until all their heads were clean. She never came back.

Kathleen was very sorry about our humiliation and very pains-taking in eradicating the pests, which was no simple matter in my mass of hair. It was cropped very short and every night Kathleen washed it in vinegar and stood over me for hours, picking nits and squashing them between her nails. I can hear the fearful snapping sound even now. I had to stay off school and when I returned the children kept their distance because my hair still stank of vinegar. It was all very embarrassing.

17 Friends and War-Work

After the news of my father's death I found the Houghton family, with its easy spontaneity, a great comfort. At that time I was being pulled in contrary directions by old and new loyalties. There was a self-imposed ritual of recalling home and parents, with all the haunting visions of my parents' sufferings that inevitably followed, and the remorse at not having written more often. Above all, there was the sheer void left by my father's death.

I longed for a prop and saw the strength Kathleen derived from Catholicism. Long talks and discussions on religion and faith became almost a daily routine with us. As we talked I realized that her religion served not only as a support, but also made harsh demands. It asked for a steely self-discipline, regular church attendance, confession, obedience and an unquestioning faith in strange concepts that were hard to swallow. The fact that rational doubt had to be fought and repressed repelled me, but at the same time I was fascinated by her powerful, all-embracing faith.

Lucy Stern reminded me of the more lucid claims of the faith that my father had held to. Inevitably I went in for a great deal of soul-searching and there were many heart-to-heart talks with Mrs Houghton, which had a marvellously catharthic effect, particularly if they ended in 'happy' tears. Mrs Houghton was wonderful at these long, introspective discussions and there was a period when they were a regular feature of Saturday morning to the puzzlement of dear, down-to-earth Mr Houghton. Mrs Houghton would leave her dusting and sweeping and even her bed-making.

'Where are you, Elsa?' Mr Houghton would call up the stairs. 'What *are* you two yarning about?'

But Mrs Houghton would give me her undivided attention. 'This is far more important than dusting. That can wait,' she called down, smiling conspiratorially and fixing me with her wide-open eyes, as though shining a torch into the dark passages of my mind, ranging with me over the issues of life and the meaning of existence. Her philosophy was sensible and consoling: she called herself a 'free-thinker' and said one didn't need to go to any church as long as one was a good person. Usually she concluded with the enigmatic admonition: 'Be kind to Hanna. Let Hanna be kind to Hanna.' I never quite knew what it meant, and didn't like to ask – it sounded so agreeable!

What I thought so marvellous in that household was the way both Mr and Mrs Houghton slaved for the happiness of their children and their children's friends. They cleaned and baked, cooked and made up 'emergency' beds on the floors of various rooms. Washing and drying, ironing, dressmaking and mending shoes, gardening and carpentry – all these jobs got done without interfering with their hospitality one bit. One was always welcome. They were never idle. If one stayed the night, one was woken late on Sunday morning with a cup of tea, brought by Mr Houghton, wandering from room to room with his tray, like a steward on a ship, at the same time informing us of the day's weather prospects.

'Sun is shining, girls! A fine day to be up and about.' Or: 'A bit grey and cool just now, but going to be fine later on.' In fact, with Mr Houghton it was always going to be 'fine later on'. He had by then already cleared away the debris of the night before, swept the carpet and probably peeled the potatoes into the bargain.

If one stayed up too late on Saturday night, reluctant to go to bed after listening to *Saturday Night Theatre* on the wireless, the evening would generally be brought to a close with the arrival of cocoa, biscuits, cheese and tomatoes. Sunday dinner was preceded by a glass of sherry, which Mr Houghton, now acting as a wine waiter, always presented with a mock bow.

I sometimes felt guilty at all the trouble that we must be giving them, but they invariably met our offers of help with, 'We like to see you all happy and enjoying yourselves.' And to my amazement, they really meant it. We did, however, all help with the dinner washing-up. It was usually Liz who suddenly got up from the table and started clattering the plates and dishes about the sink. She was very efficient and there was always quite a pile waiting on the draining board by the time the rest of us arrived. Soon the rattling of dishes was drowned by 'Green Grow the Rushes-O', 'Early One Morning' and 'Drink to Me Only'. The Houghtons were a music-loving family: both girls played the piano, and Paul (the little brother) was learning the french horn. Mrs Houghton had a full, resonant soprano voice and Mr Houghton, though very modest about exercising it, a very true, light tenor and, when pressed, he sang 'Oh Mistress Mine' most movingly. There was always singing and music-making in the house, not of the impeccable Colne House variety, but jolly, none the less. The girls sometimes played little duets and Janet, with intense concentration, could get most of the way through the first movement of the 'Moonlight Sonata' before getting stuck. Mrs Houghton would suddenly launch out with operatic fervour on 'One Fine Day' until the girls would call out in embarrassment, 'Oh Mum!' secretly rather proud of her. Mrs Houghton was delighted when Kathleen later on invited her to the Colne House concerts.

Mr Houghton's other talent was the ability to slice bread more thinly than anyone else. The slices curled delicately like autumn leaves and the butter (a cunning wartime mixture of butter and milk whipped by hand for hours) squeezed through the little holes.

Mrs Houghton's wartime tea-table had to be seen to be believed: the table, with its leaves out, seemed to sag with the load of plates of sandwiches of imaginative variety, of date buns and nut cakes, sponges made with reconstituted eggs, and home-made biscuits. This, in wartime with stringent rationing, was quite a feat. It was terribly tempting to try something of everything, particularly when, holding back discreetly, one was urged on.

Mrs Houghton, a vegetarian by upbringing and conviction, was infinitely creative in devising interesting sandwich-fillings: there might be grated cheese with Marmite, or grated cheese with grated swede – surprisingly palatable – date spread, or

Suenut spread. Equally intriguing for me were the vegetarian lunches: Nutteline loaves or Nutmeat rissoles, always served with salads and large potatoes baked in their jackets, followed by fruit pies made from brown flour. With all this there was a delicious apple drink, concocted from apple-peelings and golden syrup (which wasn't rationed, though hard to get). One always rose from the table well satisfied.

Mrs Houghton had an unshakeable faith in some potions and pills called Wallace Specifics made by Heath & Heather, and also in the beneficial effects of daily exercises. If any of us complained of stomach-ache, headache, colds and sore throats, period pains or pimples, Mrs Houghton was always ready with one of the many Heath & Heather cures ranged in her cupboard. If one chanced to walk in through the back door unannounced, one might find her stretching her spine from a door jamb or the stairhead, or waving her legs in the air from behind the dining-room table. 'Bernard Shaw does his daily exercises still, and he is well into his eighties,' Mrs Houghton justified herself if one looked astounded.

The cheerfulness and warmth of the Houghtons brought us round to Tyburn Way whenever we had the chance, so much so, that sometimes Auntie complained. 'You are practically living with the Houghtons. You really must cut down on your visits there. Besides, think of the rationing.'

We assured her that Mrs Houghton *really* didn't mind.

'Why don't you ask them to come and play here?' Kathleen suggested. But it never was the same. Janet and Liz were always on their best behaviour and sat tongue-tied on the edge of their chairs at tea-time, waiting to be offered things from the trolley and anxiously balancing plates on their laps. Besides, for me the fun lay in being part of the Houghton family.

At school I was working hard by now, for it was very important that I should get my School Certificate – apart from everything else I owed it to Lucy, who had been paying for my schooling all this time.

Eventually the time of the examinations came. The only papers I can remember anything of are those for botany and mathematics. In botany we had the usual task of identifying a flower; a sort of detective game, moving from clue to clue. The difficulty about that was that if one made a single mistake – say, about the number of stamens, or the arrangement of petals – everything else was thrown out and one might end up with a sunflower instead of a daisy! On this occasion we were all intently dismembering a pale green, weed-like flower with our razor blades and tweezers, peering through our magnifying glasses and poring over our 'Floras'. Eventually I came up with the unlikely name of 'Wood Germander' and doubtfully wrote it down. There wasn't time to start again; besides, the little plant lay in tatters. But it turned out to be right and whenever I see it now, growing insignificantly in the woods, I salute it affectionately.

The maths paper was my greatest bugbear. One *had* to pass that to get a Certificate: no amount of credits and distinctions in other subjects would compensate. We sat in the hall and I stared blankly at the geometry problems. I tried various questions, but knew, even as I did so that I was doomed to failure. I sat, biting my pen in despair.

Then I remembered Mother Gabriel's admonition: 'If you are in trouble during the examinations, remember you can always pray to St Jude.'

There seemed to be a saint for every eventuality and St Jude, we had been told, looked after 'the impossible'. Providence had, in fact, placed a small statue of St Jude in that very room. So while everyone else pored over their papers, I fastened my gaze on the brightly coloured plaster figure and prayed furiously.

Perhaps it was a revelation, or perhaps it was simply that in praying I had distanced myself from the questions and could see the wood for the trees. 'If I get all the theorems right I might scrape through, even with all the problems wrong,' I thought and set to in the short time that remained. I worked with great concentration. Janet had drilled me well in theorems; all I had to do was to decide which theorem applied to which problem.

It worked and I passed – barely – but that was all that was needed. In the other subjects I had in fact passed well enough to get my exemption from the 'matric'. Everyone was very pleased with me, including Mother Fulbert!

Now the time for deciding what to do for a living was upon me. Uncle Max, when he heard of my father's death, had without hesitation taken on himself the financial responsibility for our welfare. He had already been sending periodic drafts of money to the Salmons, but now he took his position as foster parent very seriously. He took to writing to us regularly in a funny, rather old-fashioned Mark Twain style with lovingly worded precepts for life. He would dearly have liked us to live with him in America as his 'daughters' – he himself had never had any children. Later I learned that he was sadly disappointed when we opted to stay in England, but he never put any pressure on us to change our minds.

On no account must you give up your ambitions on my account [he wrote]. I am fearful lest you pick up anything that comes along – because I am old and not earning vast sums. I have written to Mrs Salmon to do the very best for you as far as good food and clothes are concerned, and to let me know the approximate outlay for my gifted girls. I still hope to face the gladsome task of fathering Adölfl's girls, at least for long enough to see you two launched into safe channels. By the way, seeing you are *women*, I have a wee surprise for you. My friend, Mrs Baker, has been able to procure for me two evening dresses in the sizes we guessed would be right, if not, an alteration is easy . . .

These dresses, when they arrived, were like magic gowns flung upon astonished Cinderellas. Like everyone else in Britain, we were used to 'make do and mend' and 'austerity'.

These dresses, as we drew them out of the rustling tissue paper, expanded into layers and layers of frothy tulle, pure white for Lotte and almond-pink for me. They had daringly low neck-lines and airy folds of gossamer floated over the shiny taffeta underskirt, which tumbled from the figure-hugging bodices to the ground. We were enraptured – but where, oh *where* was the occasion for wearing them?

More practically, now that I had left school, Uncle Max paid my fees for a year's secretarial course at the Regent Street Polytechnic. After that, since I was eighteen, I was eligible for National Service. Harold Abrahams suggested that my fluent German would be useful at the Ministry of Economic Warfare at Lansdowne House. I applied, was interviewed by a panel of civil servants, was appointed, and invited to take an oath to abide by the Official Secrets Act. Thereafter, whenever anyone asked me what I was doing, I could justifiably answer: 'Sorry, can't say – it's hush-hush,' which made me feel very important. I commuted from Rickmansworth to London daily, which, during the days of the V1s and V2s, was often very exciting.

By now Kathleen was often not too well. Her attacks of asthma became more severe and the periods when she had to go to bed for a few days became more frequent. She seldom went out now, unless it was to church or an occasional tea-party. She spent much time reading, writing letters and occasional poems.

For a few weeks she went to a nursing home in the Banbury Road, Oxford, and occasionally Auntie went down to visit her. I think Kathleen enjoyed the change and her letters to us showed she missed us. Auntie started treating me as an adult and told me to take care of the place during her absence, which greatly pleased and flattered me. Kathleen returned a little better, but the improvement did not last long. Yet, she was always calm and understanding, ready to listen and advise, but many a time I had to leave her room suddenly when she reached for her atomizer and started fighting for breath. She never liked us to see her helpless.

Gradually she became more emaciated and frail and soon atomizers were no longer enough. Oxygen cylinders became part of the furniture of her room. Father Evariste came once a week to give her Communion, and her faith seemed to give her strength to face the terrible reality of what was happening. I greatly admired her courage, but could not bear to see her suffering so uncomplainingly. Auntie chafed dreadfully at her own helplessness. I believe that in those days she derived some comfort from our company and some distraction from our needs and activities.

For me 1945 had been an eventful year during which I had moved into the grown-up world and become more at ease with people. Wartime London was still exhilarating and I made some good friends. But at the end of the year I resigned from the Ministry. Shortly after VE Day the members of my section had been told that it was being transferred to Germany as part of the headquarters of the allied occupation. All of us were given the opportunity to go, and I had to decide whether or not to accept. It was not an obvious choice. I was earning quite well, with good prospects for a career in the Civil Service, but I could not face returning to Germany. The death of my father, and probably my mother, was still too raw a wound for me to contemplate meeting their murderers.

My time at the Ministry had constituted National Service, and so I was eligible for a grant for further education. I decided to try for a place at London University. I think everybody at the Ministry understood my reasons for not wanting to go to Germany. They gave me good references and wished me luck, and my immediate boss, Miss Petersen, gave me a signed copy of Ralph Waldo Emerson. 'You may find his outlook on life helpful,' she said, adding, 'if I were you I should take up golf.'

Instead I took up Latin. I needed School Certificate Latin to qualify for the English Honours course. After furious mugging-up of gerunds and ablatives and unseen translations I sat the exam in June, and on 26 July, when I went to get the mail for Lotte's birthday, I found the envelope I had addressed to myself. I brought the letters through and held out the envelope.

'Open it, quick!' Both Auntie and Lotte stood waiting. I *couldn't* open it. To delay the moment of disappointment and hang on to hope just a *little* longer I went into the garden. Then prepared for disaster I returned and opened the envelope. But I had passed.

18 Voices from Another Country

After the war both Uncle Max and my London cousins contacted all the various bodies that were then active in tracing missing people, to try and find out what had happened to my mother. Now and then there was a flicker of hope, though I could not bear the thought of all she must have suffered if she were still alive. By now the nature of the extermination camps was known and hideous stories of atrocities, including experiments on prisoners, were emerging and my imagination plagued and racked me again at nights. There never has been any information about my mother. We only know that in the camps she was sent to nearly everyone died in the gas-chambers.

But bit by bit we were able to fill in a little of my parents' last two years in Düsseldorf. They lived under appalling strain, their laborious efforts at emigration were thwarted one after the other. People like my father, too elderly to start afresh, and unwilling to depend on others, had delayed too long. The war had closed frontiers. As the German armies occupied country after country, sailings from neutral ports became fewer and avenues of escape were cut off, one by one. The countries to which escape was still possible were naturally unwilling to receive people without means of support, and on top of all this my parents' letters reveal that German officialdom was inefficient or deliberately obstructive, or both.

The letters they wrote to my relatives in America during 1940 and 1941 – which took up to four months to arrive and which we did not see till years later – show something of their desperate efforts and their incredible persistence in hoping, against all the odds, that they would eventually be reunited with us. Throughout there is a terrible refrain of anxiety at lack of news of their children, trapped in a Britain that they supposed was being 'blitzed' out of existence.

In July 1940 my father wrote to Uncle Hugo (the wine-merchant, now kitchen-labourer in Baltimore). The letter speaks of their affidavits, bank credentials and statement of resources, all apparently required by the US Consulate in Stuttgart.

> . . . but as long as even *one* document is lacking, Stuttgart will not summon us, and we still need a tax-statement and a declaration from Walter, stating in what manner he is going to support us, and – what is more time-consuming than everything else – we need evidence from those people for whom Walter has already stood guarantor, that they no longer need his support. So far we have yours only, and he stood guarantor for so many . . .

Then an outburst:

> *A propos* the children: is there *no one*, neither you, nor Max, Rosel or Helene, who have the imagination to realize that there are sitting in Düsseldorf parents whose need for news of their so young children, whom they know to be in great danger, has become a physical craving! You have denied us *any* news of them for more than two and a half months. It would be so simple for you to begin your letters with: 'On such and such a date we received news from Rosel (or Helene), dated so-and-so – all are well and fit, the children are together.' That's all; we don't need more than that, but we *cannot* and cannot get anyone to do this for us – it is quite incomprehensible to me. And for that reason our hearts are forever sinking to our feet. So *please please*!! . . .
>
> You do realize that by now the only way to the USA is via Asia–Japan–San Francisco . . .?

His next letter reveals that the two and a half months without news of us was to extend to four months and to drive my parents to extremes of anxiety. All this time they were subjected to exaggerated reports of the devastation of Britain and to assurances that the invasion of the British Isles was imminent.

I do not know why the letters from America gave so little news of us. This was the time when Tante Rosel was instructing us to write circumlocutory messages that could be sent via the USA, but perhaps our efforts were too long or too indiscreet for sending on. But there was no reason why my relations' letters should not have given news of us. They were kept fully informed. Tante Gretel, who acted as postmistress (since Uncle Max was always travelling on business) seems to have been quite unimaginative, often wasting precious pages on petty complaints about other members of the family and friends who were now living in America. Even when she sent news of us to my parents, it was excessively sparse and only added as an afterthought:

Your letter today, dated 3 September 1940, has satisfied our longing that has grown into torture during the last *four* months, for we have been without direct or indirect news of the children since *April*. You mention in the margin of your letter that you received a letter from Egon, dated 30 July, stating that the children are still with the doctor's family, that both are well and that Hannele is to go to a High School. . .

Please, dear Hugo, write to Rosel, Inge and Egon a letter conveying the urgent necessity for them to keep you informed of the children's and their own welfare.

They agonized over whether we should risk the U-boats and go to America at once to await them there:

The danger for the children has increased considerably during the last few weeks and will continue to do so, and now we find ourselves in the terrible and insoluble dilemma: which danger is the greater for them, to travel to the USA with Helene and Max Zippert [Tante Gretel's sister and brother-in-law who were in London waiting for their passage] or to remain with their doctor's family? The decision can only be made by those over there – we can only worry and trust in God . . .

They drew great comfort from knowing that we were at the Salmons' and from the news of Lucy's generosity:

That there are still such good people who take strange children to the extent of sending them to a High School is moving and very comforting. I can imagine how proud Hannele must feel. Are the children in spite of this still *together* at the doctor's family?

. . . If the children want to wait till we get to Uncle Max, that could take a very long time. The consulates deal with only very few cases now for emigration to the USA and apparently accept only those with particularly high guarantees or large cash credits over there – which is not the case with us. But nevertheless we continue our efforts ceaselessly, supported by Max and cousin Walter, to get out. Only last week we received a cable from Max stating, 'Passage money assured. Documents on the way. Write your intentions regarding mode of transportation.' Naturally we should accept the route via Japan, if it is still operating by the time it is our turn. Whether, in the meantime, other possibilities will occur – perhaps via Lisbon – who knows? At any rate, we are doing *everything possible* towards getting out and joining my brothers over there to start a new existence . . .

Else is, at present, taking a language course on top of all her other courses . . .

Some time after the war, when postal services between Britain and Germany were restored, Lotte and I received a letter from Hella Röttger, the wife of my father's dear friend Karl. She was still living in Gerresheim and told us that Karl had died, utterly disillusioned, six months after hearing of my father's death. Her daughters, Gerda and Rotraud, had qualified in chemistry and medicine and were married, or about to marry. Helmut, the only son, had been called up into the *Wehrmacht* and was still a prisoner of war in the East.

She told us that she and Karl had spent several evenings with my parents just before their deportation, despite the risk. Afterwards they had rescued a few things that they were keeping for us. The house in the Sonnbornstrasse was still standing undamaged and the people who had made the forced purchase and who had denied my parents shelter in the cellars during the early air-raids were still living there.

The letter linked two worlds: the present, and the remembered world of before 1939 that was already beginning to seem like a dream. We wrote back at once, begging for more news.

Frau Röttger's next letter was full of her pleasure that things had turned out so well for us in the end. She said that my parents had had very sparse news of us from the USA until 1941. They had been comforted to hear that we were happy with the Salmons. As for my intention to go into teaching (I still hankered to be a foreign correspondent, but my university grant bound me to teach) my father would have been delighted, she wrote:

You know that he himself would like to have studied for the teaching profession. He was a born teacher, combining his love for young people with a love for knowledge, and he had the rare gift for transmitting this love to other people. He often spoke about the unspeakable happines that you two had given him, and he was looking forward to the time when he could learn and work with you. Well, for a little while he was able to join in your learning, but you were separated at far too early a stage to get the full benefit of his gifts . . .

I remember well how proudly he read your essays to us, and when you were already in England he read some of your letters too, proudly noting your stylistic improvements, dear Hannele. I am not surprised that you would like to become a writer – the tendency is inherited from your father. But you are quite right not to make it your main occupation . . .

Right at the end Gerda and Rotraud begged your father for a passport photograph of himself. Your father was worried on their behalf in case the photos might endanger them, if they were found in their possession. But the girls carried them about in their wallets throughout the war, together with photographs of us and Helmut. They revered your father deeply; he served them as an example. But your mother too we loved and admired, particularly during the last years, when she was separated from you. She was so brave and took up all sorts of courses in order to earn her living abroad. She worked harder than ever before in her life and quite forgot her ailments. She grew in strength. She persevered with her English lessons and was looking forward to the day when her two children would be her teachers . . .

We learnt recently that the Fleischhacker family managed to get out to America in 1940. Do you remember Mr Heidenheim, the old Jewish gentleman who lived by himself at the bottom of our road? He was due for deportation as late as September 1944, but he had hidden himself away in his house until the British arrived in Düsseldorf on 17 April 1945. Not a soul knew about it. During those last heavy bombings and artillery attacks no one seemed to trouble. Although his house was badly damaged during one of these attacks, he remained hidden away, unharmed.

At the bottom of the letter Rotraud, the youngest daughter, wrote a few lines of greeting, telling us that she would try to get a copy made of the last passport photograph of my parents and send it to us.

When I next write I will tell you this and that about your parents. I just want to say this today: you can be very proud of your parents. For me your father always was an example and a prototype of the best and noblest in man. He was so good, so generous and kind – a truly great man, whom I loved deeply . . .

It was comforting to hear these things said about my parents, particularly as sometimes I was afraid that I idealized the memory of my father to the point of falsification. About this time we also received letters from Frau Berg and Marlies in Belgium, from friends and distant cousins in America, all of them expressing the same sentiments of admiration and love for my father, telling us of all the help he had given them when they were trying to emigrate. I knew then that he must indeed have been remarkable.

My parents had still not given up hope by September 1941, but despair was very near. Letters now took nearly half a year, if they arrived at all, and their isolation – the yellow star exposing them to humiliations and indignities on the street and the loss of contact with friends – must have been terrible. In her last letter to America, started on 25 August, 1941, my mother wrote:

At times I am so terribly tired in the evenings that I fall asleep while writing. I am constantly on the move. Apart from housework and shopping, which take up a great deal of time [it may have been difficult for her to find shops willing to serve her], I am now taking classes in massage and English too, but I am glad that I have these to take my mind off things and to keep me from coming to myself, particularly since our emigration affairs don't seem to be *working out at all*. I wonder what was the enclosure to which you refer in your last letter – would it be from Richard's Hanna, or from my Hannele? I suppose it wasn't acceptable? I will have to be content with what you have to tell us concerning the children. I wonder how Lotte's twelfth birthday went off? Adölfl's birthday was spent *gemütlich* in the company of Ada's old mother and Adele's mother, both of whom Adölfl looks after, now that their families have gone. It was very sad that he had to forego the children's letters, which is very bitter. Perhaps you could instigate that the children send us a Red Cross letter, so that we can at least see their writing, or even only their signatures.

The letter was not posted then, for on 17 September my father added:

I have been carrying this letter around with me almost a whole month, but because of all the worries and upsets I have been so churned up inside, that I couldn't bring myself to add my greetings. During the last few days we have quickly made a few, last, hurried journeys, since from now on this, too, will no longer be possible for us. I went to Essen and Cologne concerning our emigration, and yesterday I visited the graves of Margot and Bernhardt in Sohlingen, and tomorrow I shall go to Dortmund to my father's and Friedrich's graves. Else had her massage examination today in Cologne, which she passed well, but she had been working very hard for it. If she will ever be able to use it? It does *not* look like it, since the closure of the consulates, shortly before we received our passage on a boat, prevented . . .

The letter ends here and was never finished. It was not posted until 2 October 1941, about the time that my parents heard they were to be deported on the eighteenth. My father simply scribbled in the margin: 'I'll just send it off like this.' Matters had evidently now passed beyond words.

Postscript

In fact, it was not the closure of the consulates that finally prevented my parents' escape. Frau Röttger explained that in the end a ship was sailing for Cuba and at last all the documents, visas and guarantees were ready, and the tickets bought. But *Ortsgruppenleiter* Wesch was not prepared to see my parents get away.

Two days before the ship was due to sail my parents were called before the local authorities and told that my mother could not leave without an *Arbeitsbefreiungsausweis* (a certificate exempting her from war-work) since she was under the age of forty-five. The certificate had to come from Berlin and could not be obtained in time. The ship sailed without them.

The certificate was almost certainly a pretext to prevent their leaving since, in any case, Jews were not eligible for war-work. While they were anxiously waiting for this certificate, Wesch saw to it that their names were on the list for the very first deportation from Düsseldorf. They were the only ones to go from Gerresheim.

Hella Röttger's account continues:

> . . . When your mother learnt that they were to be on the first train load, she pleaded with your father that they should take their own lives (as many had done in Düsseldorf). Your father himself told us this. He calmed her and put it to her that they

should not do so, as they might still be of use to someone. She then became completely calm and brave. On their last evening – they were to be collected very early at 5 a.m. the next morning – she was completely composed and calm.

One must not forget either, that your father believed, like many people did in those days, that they were being deported into ghettos, where they might live and work and that at the end of the war they would go free. Your father spent his last money on medical supplies. The rabbi had advised that deportees should take *some*, but your father took a whole caseful, not only for his and your mother's use, but, he said, it would come in useful for all the others who were being deported with them. They were picked up on 18 October 1941. We learnt later that the men and women were separated soon after their arrival at the concentration camp of Lodz.

When it was certain that your parents were being deported, my husband, who had to go on a lecture tour, said goodbye to your father at the Lindemann archives before going. Your father gave him the address of your Uncle Max, promising to let us have news if possible. Two cards did come from Lodz to your grandparents, who were still living in your flat. In them your father asked them to send money. We arranged with Gustav Lindemann to send a little money every fourteen days through your grandparents. Later Lindemann worried, feeling that it might have been possible to hide your parents in Bavaria on his estate after all. But your father went to Lodz fully aware of what he was doing. He believed he might be able to help many people there.

In May 1942 the money was returned with a notification that Adolf Zürndorfer had died of heart-failure. Your grandparents were deported much later to Theresienstadt, where they both died.

Investigations as to my mother's fate met with a complete blank. My mother was just forty-one when she was deported, and my father was sixty-seven when he died.